WaterWrites

A HUDSON RIVER ANTHOLOGY

In Celebration of
The Hudson 400

Laurence Carr: Chief Editor and Project Co-ordinator

Nancy Lautenbach: Project Co-ordinator

Joann Deiudicibus: Poetry Associate Editor

Penny Freel and Rachel Rigolino: Memoir Associate Editors

Codhill Press
New Paltz, New York
2009

This book is published by Codhill Press,
David Appelbaum, Publisher

First Edition

Printed in the United States of America

Copyright © 2009 by Laurence Carr

ISBN-13: 978-1-1930337-43-5

Edited by Laurence Carr, Joann Deiudicibus, Rachel Rigolino and Penny Freel.
Text design by Laura Kniffen, Design and Printing Services, SUNY New Paltz
Cover Image by Morgan Gwenwald

Preface
by Laurence Carr, editor

One of my favorite Scenic Hudson walks is through the Black Creek Preserve. Down the path, over the wooden footbridge, then up and over the dappled hill, then down the winding path. You can sense the Hudson River long before you see it and see it long before you're close enough to appreciate the full extent of its power, grace, and hypnotic chants. The wind and waves create an ancient song, a river song, older than our time. A song similar to other river songs throughout the world, but unique to this place in Eastern New York.

Later, watercraft added their rhythmic accents. Paddles, the flutter and whip of sails, the dip and drip of sternwheelers, the spurt of steam, the chug of pistons, then the race of motors, with each new version a nod to progress or at least to progression. The cast and haul of nets bringing in the day's catch when the river fed a nation. The songs of work and play. The slap of waterskis.

Standing at this mid-Hudson sanctuary, my mind's eye wanders. It floats upstream (one of the few places in the world you can, on a river that flows two ways) to its place of beginning, the source of all this richness. Tear of the Clouds, high in the Adirondacks. Tear of birth, tear of joy. A river that begins with a thought, and then a drop, and then another. Drop by drop it begins its meander south, gathering itself for its journey. It pauses briefly at lakes, cuts through mounds of glacial rock, sweeps under bridges. It holds our Native heritage, the first people of the river; our Dutch heritage from Rip Van Winkle to Spyten Dyvil, our Spitting Devil; our French heritage of the Huguenots in Niewe Pfaltz; our African-American heritage trail of the Underground Railroad; our heritage of British, German, Irish and Italian immigrants who fished and shipped and built a nation from its currents.

It flows past the memories of Native American settlements, past the homes of wealth and the homes in debt, past the Temples of Commerce and the sooty factories, past palaces and clamsheds, past Vanderbilt and Roosevelt. Past scenes captured ten thousand times on canvas after canvas by Cole and Church, by Bierstadt, Cropsey and Gifford, and their school of followers, past and present. It flows past Dia Beacon and Storm King, the home to artists who seek the essence of today in steel and stone and glass.

It flows past West Point, past soldiers of all stripes and decoration. The Hudson has seen them retreat, advance, find themselves, find their course, and find their country in the glinting sparkle of its water. It flows past Sing Sing, past those who wear another uniform, past those who've lost their way and see something else in the water's reach. It flows around the island where Bannerman's Castle stands, built to house our might, now a romantic commuter curiosity.

It's a river that remembers a day in 1609, when it first saw sails and discovered the miniature *Half Moon*, that little floating box of wood and canvas, rope and iron, glass and men that the river could lift with one strong wave. A river that wondered what these people from so far away were thinking and what brought them to these waters. The Dutch, the French, The British sailed up and down its current, each a passing storm to these waters of another name, and just as much a curiosity from those native people, the first who learned its tides.

There was a time within the memories of many when the Hudson was lost in a fog of greed and many thought that wealth could be stacked in darkened rooms or in glowing electronic files. Pollution, disregard, the hubris of humankind. We lost the wealth that flowed before us.

But even in these dark days, there were those who illuminated the manuscripts and maps that would show us the way out. Slowly, we came to see the Hudson for what it always was. Our friend and teacher who would never leave us. We need to let the Hudson guide us. Let it remain one of the main arteries that flows life to us and through us, from the Tear of the Clouds, the tear of joy that celebrates its creation to its New York City mouth that brashly speaks our past and present, and if we listen, will speak our future.

Many thanks to all who keep the Hudson River as part of their lives, especially to Pete Seeger for his steady hand in the creation of the good ship *Clearwater* and for his ongoing love and attention for this waterway. Hemingway had his "Old Man and the Sea." We are honored to have, with respect, "Our Old Man of the River."

We would also like to thank Dr. Thomas Olsen, Chair of the English Department at SUNY New Paltz for helping to bring this book together. And last but not least, we dedicate this book to all the artists of the Hudson Valley, who shape their life's work here and are inspired by this vibrant river, our Hudson.

Contents

Preface
    by Laurence Carr, editor . . . . *i*

PART I: POEMS
Poem
    Hideichi Oshiro *1*
That First Winter
    Marilyn Reynolds *2*
A Winter Hudson
    Joe Fischer *5*
Poughkeepsie in January
    Judith Saunders *7*
Mirror
    Ken Holland *8*
Salt Front (The uppermost reach of saline water in an estuary.)
    Paul R. Clemente *9*
The Hudson River in Winter
    Robert Milby *11*
"hudson river poem"
    Tyler Wilhelm *12*
Frozen Pantoum
    Jo Pitkin *13*
Year's End on the Hudson
    Bobbi Katz *14*
Dawn Breaks On Lovers
    Joanne Rose Trapanese *15*
By the River, St. Patrick's Day: Two Observations, Two Modes
    Kevin Larkin Angioli *16*
Poughkeepsie Railroad Bridge Poem (When Marie Swam Across the River)
    Thomas Doran *17*
Doing Nothing
    Barbara Adams *19*
Being and Time
    James Finn Cotter *21*
Passing by Ossining on Saturday Mornings
    Rhonda Shary *23*
Estuary
    Joann K. Deiudicibus *24*
Weightless
    Christine Boyka Kluge *25*
Thinking Spring and The Hudson
    Jim Handlin *26*
On the Waterfront
    Claudia McQuistion *28*

Scent of Lilacs
    Ethel Wesdorp *30*
Thirty-Seven Bags of Consumer Trash
    Caroline Wolfe *31*
Breakfast on the Hudson
    Meg McKay *33*
Driving West
    Maureen Waters *35*
Athens, NY
    Bob Wright *36*
Scarlet Turnings
    Mike Jurkovic *38*
Hudson Geese at Sunset
    Donna Sherman *39*
Life is Worth Living
    James Sherwood *40*
Between
    Lucia Cherciu *41*
Haiku Flow
    Patricia Martin *42*
Shad Run
    Marion Menna *43*
The river runs through IT
    Abigail Robin *44*
Stealin' Blueberries
    Thomas Perkins *45*
Fragment On Water
    Donald Lev *46*
The Distant Catskills
    Robert H. Waugh *48*
Good Ground and Sweet Wood
    William Seaton *49*
The Savior Fails New York City
    Andrew Higgins *51*
Crossing
    Colin Jones *53*
Low Tide
    Allen C. Fischer *54*
On Overlook Mountain with the Rock Reader
    Annajon Russ *56*
In Between
    Michael Lutomski *58*
Rose Petals Falling in the Grand Canyon: Wallkill River View
    Jan Zlotnik Schmidt *59*
Painting
    Lynne Digby *60*

PART II: MEMOIR AND ESSAY

The Hudson
Odessa Elliott 63
Center Stage: Revolutionary African Combatants in the Hudson River Valley
(from the book *Long Hammering*)
A. J. Williams-Myers 65
The Hudson River Swim
Barbara Freer 69
Ring Of Fire
Werner Hengst 71
Maverick Memories
Anthony Robinson 74
My Hudson River
Judy Mage 76
Family Album
Howard Winn 79
Tashlikh-On-Hudson
Amelia B. Winkler 82
Westward Crossing
Penny A. Freel 84
Memoir
Jonathan M. Freiman 86
Cowheads
Nancy O. Graham 88
River Generations
Madeline Mazzetti Labriola 91
Rivers and Bridges I Have Known
Janet Neipris 93
The Hudson
Mary Armao McCarthy 96
A Sea Change on the Hudson
Betsy McCully 99
Poems Paddled Down the Hudson
Pam Mitchell 102
The River Rats, 1973
Jack Murphy 105
Hudson River Reminiscence
Chelsea Whitaker 107
My River
Linda J. Still 109
Not Henry Hudson
Sonia T. Lynch 111
Author Biographies 113

PART I POEMS

Poem

Hideichi Oshiro

River Hudson flows
   up, mist or fog
  down, rain or snow
in and out our breath.

That First Winter

Marilyn Reynolds

I knew

as I crawled (to avoid a fall)   from my car   across

the expanse of ice   towards my cottage in the woods

grounded   my knees raw

to be especially attuned   to the silence

knowing that it was aware of the secrets I hid

In this aloneness

within my first winter in the Valley

I would discover the link

between isolation and truth

and not regret it

Moving up here from Manhattan

was not a difficult decision

I belonged in the woods

had longed for years

to turn this page

Now winter held me in its hand

beholden to my electric blanket

the house having no heat   no running water

I welcomed this barebone existence

offering myself to the unknown   a common theme in my life

(after all   hadn't my ancestors crossed the plains in covered

wagons

lanterns swinging as they made circles in the snow?)

Inside my shelter

having gutted the floor to insulate

I walked across planks to get to bed

after work   eating quick suppers out

taking showers at friends

climbing into a warm bed with a book

looking out into the night sky

I felt safe to open the pain of my childhood

set it loose to the stars

(One night I was awakened by a translucent man   khaki pants

white shirt

reddish hair   freckles

standing at the foot of my bed

Why are you here? I asked   surprised   but feeling no fear

Just wanted to make sure you were ok   *he responded*   *with*

a gentle smile

And then he vanished)

In the heart of my igloo

there is the softness of my cloak of forgiveness/the kitten

that has come in from the cold to sleep with me 'til dawn

there are comforting voices

(that screamed in the past)

kneeling in supplication in my alabaster bowl   we breathe

crystalline frost

together

(the night is never longer than when I search in open space

for my familiar

star to sit upon   it was right here yesterday   I say to myself

in the hallowed stillness and careless breeze   I stumble upon

it   silly me)

Now

before it's too late

turn your head away from time

there is no such thing

Let it snow!

A Winter Hudson

Joe Fischer

I woke late and cloudy
The frosted windows
Milling slowly
Cleaning frenzy
Away from home,
Christmas comes a few days early

Rinsing party crumbs
from almost empty cocktail glasses
Sleep-eyed, packing clothes and presents
Double checking railroad passes

Stuffed inside a shuttle bus
Short days: 5 looked like 11
Stepped onto that ancient bullet
Outdated and out of fashion

As the rough tracks rock the train
The Hudson to the right
I stare
Sit by the doors that open with
The burst of frozen river air

Electric light feels out of place
against the early darkened sky
It reflects, and I time-travel, back to 1965

The Hudson River came and went
My TV screen was window glass
Sometimes water
Sometimes stars
The moon, and then the castle, passed

The winter storm
The freezing snow
I watch the thick ice float in schools
They decorate the river
Beaming
Out-of-focus, alien blue

The bridges that connect the land
above the wide and cresting water
Mark the ride unconsciously
Mid-Hudson to the Tappan Zee

This is not a midnight trip
I trick myself and then remember:
'There's nowhere else that this could be
than Metro-North in late December.'

Poughkeepsie in January

Judith Saunders

This is the season

    that subtracts and deletes,

        acknowledging topography.

Erasing autumn's brushy tangles

    of grass and weed and vine,

        whole canopies of foliage,

emptying space

    between orchard and pond,

        winter runs a chalky finger

along the river's edge,

    flattens its waters

        with a dull-white thumb,

seizes trees as pencil-sticks

    to trace sharp lines

        up and down, up and down

the mountainous banks

    of the ice-bound Hudson,

        insisting on contours

            the summer will obscure.

Mirror

Ken Holland

The Hudson secludes its way
past West Point
Academy of discipline,
set up the bluff
as improbable as
a Fragonard fantasy,
in wonderment
at its own reflection.
While the river
urges its waters
to slip quietly along,
furtive and breathless,
like felons breaking prison.

Salt Front (The uppermost reach of saline water in an estuary.)

Paul R. Clemente

Salinity makes its morning commute down river,
urged on by the slacking tide, and a tail-wind of freshwater;

the saltwater returns mid-day, by the force of the moon,
like a periodic geothermal reaction where the geyser is
so reliable they can build a tourist attraction around it.

A Coast Guard cutter keeps the shipping lanes clear of ice.

At the helm, the ship's captain tries to imagine what it takes for
a river to pierce a mountain range.

Forces so methodical or catastrophic that
native lore trumps science.

Where the sudden draining of an inland sea, or
retreating mile-high glaciers, are so intangible
that who would deny that the Highlands were once a
hibernating bear family covered in snowdrifts;

awoken by an eagle's cry and the scent of a sturgeon in the
bird's talons; the bodies of the waking bears held the banks
of a great thawing lake;

the bear family, famished from their winter's sleep,
swatted at the eagle. The startled eagle dropped
the fish into the icy shallows of the lake; the sturgeon felt revived;

seeing that the bears and the eagle were moving rapidly toward him,
the powerful sturgeon jumped, with a thunderous slap of his tail,
over the top of
the squabbling bears and eagle, dragging the lake water though the

mountains via the now vacated bear den and landed in the ocean.

From then on the river flowed to the ocean. The plentitude and strife
of the sea making its way inland, upriver. The salt front had begun.

The Hudson River in Winter

Robert Milby

Morning Hudson River has ice on its face;
Ice on its skin in late January.
Ghosts fly low to kiss ice bouquets in its powerful arms, jeweled
cloak;
Hair rivulets and tribulations of Winter blue.

I shout crow poetry from a sleep deprived bridge in auto thunder,
Thinking of Parisi and his darkened theatre.
Considering restraint before the sunrise,
Yet remembering the brevity of human existence
And yearning for the warm freedom of my beautiful lover's
embrace.
She shall leave and return, leave and return—a river of emotional
Power, a capsized boat carried far away.
Yet in this river, there is magic.
Logs return, gulls return, eagles introspect introverted hawks.
Currents of human struggle.

We are ensnared in the satraps of poisoned modernity.
We beat conundrums of confusion and confession.
And the river is a witness to our fervor; a mirror to our passion,
A quiet repository of grief, of joy, of mystery, and constancy.

And will you drag the psychic river of your thoughts—turbulent
flow
Of dream fragments or simply drive over the bridge, never pausing,
Repeating the turgid commute into older age when blood cools
And fears are kept like animal husbandry or pets nestled by the
hearth?

I do not wish to marry Lethe or the foggy regrets of my past.
But I shall follow ghosts, curiously, until they no longer have ice on
their faces.

"hudson river poem"

Tyler Wilhelm

they say I've lived
in Catskill my whole life
I believe it

I know I've never swum in the Hudson River
but I can clearly remember a time
when I took the chance
and
ate something out of that dark water

Spat out the bones

Frozen Pantoum

Jo Pitkin

What never happens happens
one long span of winter,
the channel of open water
crusts, folds in, scars over.

One long span of winter,
the river is a bone-colored thread:
it crusts, folds in, scars over
despite salt and tides.

The river is a bone-colored thread
we want to witness together.
Despite salt and tides,
cold changes the familiar narrows.

We want to witness. Together,
walls of the gorge lock with ice.
Cold changes. The familiar narrows.
Wind whittles down my voice.

Walls of the gorge lock with ice
between Crow's Nest and Bull Hill.
Wind whittles down my voice.
Swans strut on hidden swells.

Between Crow's Nest and Bull Hill,
a frozen passage seams the land.
Swans strut on hidden swells.
I balance on the pearly chalaza of a shell.

A frozen passage seams the land
and the channel of open water.
I balance on the pearly chalaza of a shell.
What never happens, happens.

Year's End on the Hudson

Bobbi Katz

The world today is monotone
shades of gray from dark to white:
the harvest of a busy night
when snowflakes scurried from the sky
with none to count them
        none to try.

Beyond the pines
  below the hill
the silhouettes of leafless trees
reveal the river spread
      at rest
stilled, perhaps, by bitter chill.

Or maybe the river
      is busy
      instead
spinning ripples and waves
  into frozen thread
   slowly becoming
an ice-clad bed
  ready for
      blankets
      of snow.
Yes, ice-clad
and ready for snow.

Dawn Breaks On Lovers

Joanne Rose Trapanese

Night cedes a crevice

Cracks form north to south,

white birds' feet on coal;

Slate ruptures pink in the flat wall

that is the east;

Gold fissures tug open the sun,

      untangling Earth

      and the Hudson

      from sky,

      dissolving

      night's separation of us;

A spray of daylight erupts.

We are each other's epicenters;

Bold morning explodes on us

in boulders of light.

By the River, St. Patrick's Day: Two Observations, Two Modes

Kevin Larkin Angioli

Praying by a river in Upstate New York,
Sharp shoots of new life in the sun on the bank,
I swear I can smell the sea.

I am the man that stands here, sun blazing between my legs. The river is my bed. The sounds, the trickles, the *cu-lunks*, the ripples roll through my head. Bird song and spring's rampant lust-chatter encircle and enliven me. I am the man in black, but spring is on my sleeves, and I came to see and I came to walk and I came to teach and I came to learn and I came to love and the prophets are all useless now. Because we have found the river and the life is here, now. The sun is alive with me here now. What is in this breeze is here to keep, as the mountains send love letters via my eyes in the afternoon.

Poughkeepsie Railroad Bridge Poem (When Marie Swam Across the River)

Thomas Doran

The trains came off into the river
like skin, but she
got it worst of all
though I
often think if I had two eyes
it could have been me instead of her;
instead of me and Kay setting
the canoe in the river as Patrick,
on the other side, watched with
binoculars. Dad was there; he
stood with Irish arms crossed,
a bottle of Thunderbird wine,
his uniform. It was 1966.

We followed Marie in the canoe.
The trusswork cast a shadow, and she
passed through it like a dead needle.
Dad stood on the shore with his arms
crossed.

I wished my glass eye would slip out
and float along.
Marie was on her back. She
was thinking about
how dad hit her across the mouth, his
hands soaked in gasoline.

The trains were coming off into the water
like stretched out bodies, slung together;
they were coming, hitting the water, and
turning into swimmers jumping off
the water onto

bridges and turning into trains with people
going out the windows and sleeping at the
bottom.

"I bet you can't swim across the river," he
said, red, three sheets, tired, 6 a.m.

We called out to her: "Okay?"
"Marie?"
"Tired?"
"Marie."

Patrick, with his binoculars, was waving.
I could see his teeth now. Kay blew him
a kiss. Dad was impossible, a speck at the
edge of the old city, and it was getting late.
He had work.
I told Kay the trains could come off, and
Marie could take them into her body and
swim them coastal.

When she came on the shore, we
were pulling up the canoe.
Her body. Patrick gave me the
binoculars, and I saw dad walking
away through the industrial
decay as if he had only stuck around
to make sure Marie would be okay.

Doing Nothing

Barbara Adams

I am sitting on a log
In quiet April green
Gnats gnarling my white hair
In a black corona.
As if I were a pheremonic goddess.

My son is climbing the mountain
With my grandchild
The icicles dripping from boulders
Into melting snow on the trail.

Ice water rushes through Split Rock
the waterfall a pillow of ice
the pool below clear as a lens.

The patch of sun moves
Leaving me in the shade of leafless trees.
A stick turns slowly
Like a second hand on a clock
In an eddy.
I take off my shoes and wade in,
my ankles burning,
and push the stick into the mainstream.
It shrugs, then flails like an amateur skier
Towards the falls.

I have moved the universe, I smile,
As an oak tree cracks and falls
Like a man shot to death,
Brushing me with stiff limbs.

Soaked from head to toe,
I climb back to my log.

"You must have been bored, waiting,"
Says my son. "It takes courage to sit still,
 I reply, "Not patience."

Being and Time

James Finn Cotter

I: *We Walk Into Our Lives*
We saw with our own eyes
On the wide landscape of Being
Light pour all afternoon
That day in April we trekked
The Shawangunk stone ridge

On Gertrude's Nose and Millbrook
Above the Hudson Valley and River
Curled gleaming in the distance
From Storm King to the Catskills
Cresting range on range before us

While we strode onward true north
All that long April afternoon
When light streamed like rain
From clouds crossing our trail
In the blue-white sky overhead

Spreading and sifting the sun
Around, over, and under us
In the broad landscape of Being
As we glimpsed through our own eyes
How we walk into our lives.

II: *We Walk Out Of Our Lives*
We felt in our own hearts
On the blazed trail of Time
Snow falling all morning
That day in December we hiked
The Highlands glacier ledge

From Mount Beacon to Break Neck
Above the Sugar Loaf gorge
Spiked with cedar and fir
Over the Hudson River and bay
Glittering with ice floes below us

While we tramped onward due south
All that brisk December day
When snow fell like sunlight
Shattered in crystals blown
In our faces, brushed by feet,

Swirling and drifting dust
Around, over, and under us
On the white ridge of Time
As we knew in our own hearts
How we walk out of our lives.

Passing by Ossining on Saturday Mornings

Rhonda Shary

True blue river
Sky reflects on your waves

The train goes by
The barbed wire

The ten-foot thick brick walls
The horrifying towers

I hope you all escape
Even you heinous ones

You ones who committed crimes
Unspeakable, unforgivable

Escape the prison of the self
You ones who are innocent

Guilt so great
That if you felt it

The sky
Could not contain it

Cruelty squashed
Into cages instead

Traveler, pass by.

Estuary

Joann K. Deiudicibus

Wide-hipped woman outstretched
for cities of men, the North River shudders
off her January jewels, ice shine
shattered smooth by bird strike.

Her wave-blown wrinkles sink
and fade, fall, then surface,
swelling tidal desire.

River of Mountains,
I drink you down like the Delaware,
walk you like the waxing Wallkill.
I row you like the Neversink.

You are my boat.

Drowned river, June blooms
perennial in tidal petals
floating on February waters.

Weightless

Christine Boyka Kluge

This morning I wear the clouds
like an Elizabethan ruff
around my neck.

My head floats above,
disembodied and of
the purest, palest blue.

Darker thoughts have wobbled off,
shooed like the dizzy, half-thawed gnats.
Even the edgy crows are strangely silent.

The river's tarnished mirror glitters.
At last my eyes are washed of winter.
A faint smile flickers
across my celestial lips,
like a smear of iridescence.

I can't see past my cumulus collar
to the colorless body below.
But somewhere my heart quivers,
invisible as a sprouting seed.
Somewhere, like bird claws,
my toes curl and relinquish the earth.

Can you see me hovering
above the maple's red haze
of splitting buds?

Untethered, I float.
It's late morning, early April.
I float.

Thinking Spring and The Hudson

Jim Handlin

when she bends to turn soil

it's spring

and there are worms

some for fishing

some for aeration

half and half the division

this part male

this part female

and the thinking about it

when the vegetables come in

the fish slow roasted

male and female he made them

and they named them

continue to name them

the male of the river and its flow

the feeling wind on water

the shimmer that is her dress

for the female of farm and land

and what pains its way into light

down that long corridor

as if down a river

and his boots next to the sink

the male of mud

and puddle

and the clean up that's him

On the Waterfront

Claudia McQuistion

Hold still
as I remember
this moment:
the wet, emerald grass

the gray silk
gathered right

behind it. Here
it is always
May,

car doors
flung open
like jaws

that cannot lose
teeth, a precious
cradle,

the miraculous body.

Even rivers rise
and fall, pebbles strive
to be rounder

firewood pines
for a name.
Our feet move

well when we walk,
our charming voices
sing, return

to the bed
which summoned them,
bidding farewell

like a lark
looking back. Do we honor
the places we spring

from? We meaure
our footprints.
We crush

April leaves.

Scent of Lilacs

Ethel Wesdorp

In early May the lilacs bloom
along the Catskill trail,
their sweet perfume still lingers there,
though there's no dwelling anywhere;
no chimney tall, no cellar deep,
just bluestone slabs beneath the trees.

Once a family struggled there
to wrest a living from the land,
their farmhouse snug along the path,
their rustic barn along the ledge.
The stream still wanders through the woods,
the family rests beneath the leaves.

All that remains are weathered dreams
and the scent of lilacs on the breeze.

Thirty-Seven Bags of Consumer Trash

Caroline Wolfe

"Who will pick this up?" I asked early last spring as
I walked along village wetlands bordering our suburban lawns
Winter's retreat had exposed plastic bottles and coffee cups to go

Since the little red hen was nowhere to be found and
"Not I" neighbors ignored it as they passed by
Cleaning up the trash seemed the right thing for me to do

Coke, Pepsi, Gatorade: Sprite, 7-Up and Mountain Dew
Dasani, Dowser, Adirondack: Evian, Aquafina, and Poland Spring
A flotilla of thirst quenchers amongst the brown reeds

"There's a lot of trash in the small stream," I told the village board
"You mean the drainage ditch?" they asked
On subdivision plans the wetlands are referred to as Retention
Ponds A & B

Tell that to the red-winged black bird who stakes his cattail territory
Or the mallard pairs who raised seven ducklings here
Call it a culvert, but the muskrat and dragonfly have another name:
home

Remnants of last year's BBQs: frayed nylon webbing separated
from its lawn chair
Styrofoam plates and ribbed plastic cups in red and blue
Checkered table cloth with an umbrella pole hole, faded Frisbee,
and a busted ball

And cans: Budweiser, Heineken, Miller Lite, Red Bull, Monster,
and Lightning Bolt
Teenagers party behind the bushes where the junco, yellow finch
and sparrow live

I find their left behind tire tracks, keg tapper, and bubble gum wrappers

Hannaford, Shop Rite, and Stop n' Shop bags thin as cellulose disintegrate in my hands
Thick-walled Scott's GrubEx sacks filled with muddy water
White flag-tattered bags wave surrender in branches at the high water mark

Swamp, ditch, storm-water runoff; culvertized, retained, and re-directed
Is still a pond, is still a stream as water flows from highland to lowland,
from wetland capillary to seasonal stream, to rock strewn creek, then river, then ocean.

Thirty-seven bags of consumer trash removed from one square mile of village wetlands
"Who will help me enjoy some clean water?" I ask.
"I will," said the salamander, the frog, and the little box turtle.

Breakfast on the Hudson

Meg McKay

The river slinks

slithers

sneaks

and quietly oozes by my window

on a gloomy Sunday morning.

Gray

like a greedy squirrel's silver tail or

an empty beach at dusk or

a corpse's face.

Smooth

like the ragged imitation satin on the corners of my

threadbare baby blanket.

They've both seen better days.

Cold

like a doctor's prodding, unfamiliar hands or

an icy snowball down my back or

a chilly August night and summer's abandon.

Deep

like cryptic poetry or

a blind man's eyes or

that ubiquitous discussion of chickens and eggs.

It steals away to the Atlantic in no particular hurry

while I eat my cornflakes and flip through

a Betty Crocker cookbook.

Driving West

Maureen Waters

Driving west toward the Shawangunk cliffs,
she fixes on a shaft of granite banking
the road as it winds under old growth hemlock.
The house is still shuttered against the snow,
November's cord of wood still heaped against
the gable. Grappling with the unfamiliar,
she will not look at fields, flowering now,
nor the sweep of the tender willow.

A muskrat flicks its tail, tips over into
the swollen pond. Red-wing blackbirds dart
singing through the rushes. But
she will not look at what he loved,
steadfast in emptiness.

Athens, NY

Bob Wright

Today the Hudson looks more

like lake than river. It's August,

and the floating docks that poke out

from the river park along the shore

are moving only slightly as the swells

from passing boats sweep up against

them. The hollow squeals we hear

as parts of them rub up and down

against each other seem quite muted,

as though the docks themselves had

long ago agreed not to disturb

the summer calmness of this place.

Two teenage girls on bikes race down

the gravel path that brings them

to the docks, dropping their bikes

onto the grassy border and racing out

to sit along the river's edge, their legs

dangling, laughing, eating from a bag

of M&M's, and looking out across the water.

How could such a summer day be better
in a small river town? It harkens back
to times when every place seemed just
like this in August.

Scarlet Turnings

Mike Jurkovic

G'morning Mohonk moon
Pale ghostface
Orchard watchman,

Tell me the secrets
You learned last night
About harvest and how

The sugar maples
Pace their scarlet turning
Towards dawn,

How an inkling of mist
From Minnewaska
Lifts my elders

Tell me ancient guardian
How the world turns.

Hudson Geese at Sunset

Donna Sherman

As though the bell was rung by the master
cushions laid out
incense lit
and the temple doors closed

They settle on the still skin of the water
wings tucked, necks folded
rising and falling
in silent repose.

Life is Worth Living

James Sherwood

Proclaims one of two rust-frilled signs placed one-eighth of a mile
in either direction across the Mid-Hudson Bridge—
statistically the likeliest spot they'll be seen
by the four people every year
who need the message most.
The call box waits
one hundred and thirty-five feet above
the glittering rippled river, dumb to
the thrum of passing tires bumping over
steeltoothed expansion joints,
whipping wind and gulls' cries.
What drives someone to this place?
The divorce, the layoff, the drugs, the voices
repeating over and over that there is
no end, no escape, the way out is down,
down, a hiss and a splash or a flat smack to
blackness.
It is one way out, but consider the phone.
The call box waits still,
the hinged door half-
open—
a welcome of sorts, an invitation . . .
a few miles away, someone sits
on the other end, drinking coffee,
hoping to talk
to you.

Between

Lucia Cherciu

Extended out
between one bank of the river
and another
from toes stretched out to tips of fingers
strained to reach across
undulating softly with the waves
baking in the sun
reverberating with the ripples of the water
shaking under the cluster of trailer trucks
and reeling after the romance of cross-
country driving

reaching deep where
fish glide their vulnerability
transparent with poisons
their fins taking in the sifting pulsations
of breath under murky waters

and up in the sky till the sun
swings in the rails

only the seagulls
remind of the persistence of light
the arduous tenacity of the bridge
arching from
shore to shore
from one homeland to another.

Haiku Flow

Patricia Martin

Lightning

Electric ribbons
luminous night sky dancing
nature slashes sky

Shaman

Porcupine shaman
hunches, quill cape quivering
whispers prayers to leaves

Shad Run

Marion Menna

Red-winged blackbirds oka-lee
from thickets of cat-tails on the shore.
Shadblow serviceberry is in bloom,
glittering white in the hedgerows.

Shad roe has burgeoned in the deeps,
fine dining for crabs and eels.
What's left over bursts forth,
gray spurts of tiny fry.

Carried by the current to the sea,
they school, and browse, and grow
until one spring, they swim upriver
to spawn where they were born.

Grown shad are bony fish,
like a porcupine inside out,
still all along the river's shores
men and boys stand with nets

drag them up onto the land
in silver struggling heaps –
the flesh is filleted from the bones
and fried in oil at makeshift stands.

In the same season, at the same time,
the shadblow glistens – perfect, star-shaped,
five-petalled flowers, a blaze of white,
as abundant as the bones, the roe, the fish.

The river runs through IT

Abigail Robin

What's the IT?
Is IT love, human compassion, mercy, the common good?
Where does the RIVER run through?
NEW YORK, Estate
WASHINGTON, Estate
How do we distribute the common wealth?
From east to west; north to south; through small towns and great
communities
WE are the RIVERS
WE flow back and forth.
WE wave up and down.
WE build cross sections of population from east to west; north to
south
Through small towns and great communities

The Pumpkin Sale
The pumpkin sale sails forth on clear waters
Education takes place on Pete Seeger's Sloop
Slooping up kindergarden ones
Who carry pumpkins of every type, shape, age,
Who can define and classify the pumpkin's skin and its shell?

We gather together to ask the landlord's blessing....
Geronimo, Livingston, Van Dyke and Rock-A-Fella

I rode on top of the river, through the river, under the river, across
the river
Carrying my pumpkin on my back, in my arms, across my lap...
top.

Stealin' Blueberries

Thomas Perkins

From the State park
Is close
As we'd like to come
To robbin' a bank.

We'd reference some TV memory

And with nonchalance,
Hidin' berry
Blood-stained hands,
Blend
In easy,
Hiker smiles,
Walk past rangers
With bellies full of blue
Butterflies.

Fragment On Water

Donald Lev

Does water fit the argument?
I see it in my palms
I feel it pouring down the back of my neck
I drink it
I bathe in it
My soul is cleansed by it
A leak some places can result in a big water bill
I stepped into a ditch filled with it, not good
Aren't we humans mostly water and a little ash?
Did I get that right?
The earth is mostly water and a little dirt
Right?
They think maybe they found some on Mars?
Like water's a big subject
Maybe too big for me to tackle
Like life, which I tackle often anyway, or
Death, about which I'm a minor expert
But this is water
This is "blood, sweat, and tears"
This is Jesus in Gethsemane sweating blood
This is the iceberg that did in the Titanic
This is the ocean out of which someone wants to
Bring up the Titanic
Whose morals are being questioned
Water and morality
Water in the mideast a big subject
I'm not equipped to discuss
I should have majored in geology in college, maybe
Gotten into hydrology
All you needed to do was memorize a bunch of rocks
I counseled my friend Rudy to do it, and he did
He's a practicing geologist today, whatever that is
I don't know whether he's a hydrologist, though

We *are* discussing water
Does that bring us to discuss skies and clouds and
Rain and snow and bridges over the Hudson and
All the ships at sea
And urine
And pus
But now I've gone too far
A nice little running brook
To delight our mind

The Distant Catskills

Robert H. Waugh

Sometimes they bulk up huge, sometimes so small
a mouse could skip across their ridges, toe
and hop it that the morning sun would laugh
to see it dance.

       Sometimes they stir in mist
an insubstantial scrim and in them move
inscrutable constructions, promises,
torsos and mouths wrapped in an autumn smoke
that laps the trees.

       Sometimes their clarity,
a murderous brilliance out of bounds, burns to
salute the sun; sometimes, the sun at last
sunken behind their shoulder, slumberous, they
let loose all being, forms and transformations
and roll down into nothing, lower than nothing,
lower than breath and lower than a heart-beat.

Good Ground and Sweet Wood

William Seaton

good ground and sweet wood and goodly oaks and walnut
and chestnut and sweet wood and good ground and sweet
wood and good ground grass and flowers and goodly trees
goodly oaks and walnuts and chestnuts and sweet wood and
good ground and sweet wood grass and flowers and
good ground and sweet wood and goodly oaks and walnut
and chestnut and sweet wood and good ground and sweet
wood and good ground grass and flowers and goodly trees
goodly oaks and walnuts and chestnuts and sweet wood and
good ground and sweet wood grass and flowers and
good ground and sweet wood grass and flowers and

oysters and beans for trifles
tobacco and wheat for love
tobacco and wheat for knives and trifles
green tobacco for beads
grapes and pumpkins for trifles
green tobacco for beads
tobacco and wheat for knives and trifles
tobacco and wheat for love
oysters and beans for trifles

good ground and sweet wood and goodly oaks and walnut
and chestnut and sweet wood and good ground and sweet

wood and good ground grass and flowers and goodly trees
goodly oaks and walnuts and chestnuts and sweet wood and
good ground and sweet wood grass and flowers and
good ground and sweet wood and goodly oaks and walnut
and chestnut and sweet wood and good ground and sweet
wood and good ground grass and flowers and goodly trees
goodly oaks and walnuts and chestnuts and sweet wood and
good ground and sweet wood grass and flowers and
good ground and sweet wood grass and flowers

This text was generated from the journal of Robert Juet who was
with Henry Hudson on the "Half Moon" in 1609. Juet was one of
the mutineers who set Hudson adrift in an open boat, presumably
to his death, only two years later. Juet then died himself just before
making it back east across the Atlantic.

The Savior Fails New York City

Andrew Higgins

The Archangel of the Palisades stares at the skyline
as cherubs dab Brut in the cleft of his chin.

He is remembering a time when DeSotos cruised
these streets and silk was the highest ambition of men.

A time when the river itself glistened in oil and the moon
hung un-trodden in the sky. These were the glory days of the
 Archangel,

days when he walked the streets dispensing salvation and grace
on the slick-backed heads of young men, pressing condoms and
 whiskey

into their open palms that slid along pleated skirts, handing Cuban
 cigars
to old men who loitered about the doorways of delis and liquor stores.

Thinking back on it now, he blames the Kennedy Administration
for bringing beauty out of the back alleys and shifting glamour

to the crude glare of Los Angeles. He thinks, "If only Nixon,

Nixon had been beautiful that night the nation watched

him sweat and darken, perhaps this could have all been avoided,

and the sky would still drift in jags of desire,

and the tug boats would still muscle along Staten Island

bringing redemption to the rough, un-calloused men."

Crossing

Colin Jones

Train tracks wind into the distance
and gravel crunches underfoot.
From the western shore
I stare at a red and orange mountain.

The swift chill river wind tousles my hair
and clicks the dry leaves together in the trees.
Their chatter echoes off the water,
adding its own voice.
I recede into the music, lost.

I will cross the bridge above to get home,
but my spirit will never forget, and never has;
between lapping river shore
and rising autumn mountainside,
this is my world.

Low Tide

Allen C. Fischer

As the tide pulls back
like a lid from an eye,
I look at the Hudson
and then at what it has left
on its sodden banks,
some of it water's debris,
some of it ours.

And for a moment, I imagine
the wake of a dead civilization –
around me its artifacts for the next
life: rope, oil cans, bottles, tires,
a broken oar, plastic drums
and rusted staves. These
mixed in with some of the river's
essentials: water chestnuts, driftwood,
dreadlocks of milfoil, silt's infinity,
here and there
the body of a dead fish.

The river has reached a low point
and doesn't seem to know what to do -
whether to cover the grave site with mud
or continue the sleaze of exposure.
Only the gulls and cormorants move
decisively, screaming out of sync with
the meditations of tide and spirit.

What I feel is the season of an animal
moulting, shedding its skin,
accepting that life's rhythm is
not its choice but controlled by something
else, that the motion of arrival and

departure, fullness and depletion,
are a kind of water music.
At this time, when I am drained
and stand alone in silence at the edge
of myself, there is nothing I can do
but wait, knowing the absence
is temporary and soon water
will come flowing back.

On Overlook Mountain with the Rock Reader

Annajon Russ

1.

On the summit, our fingers trace lines

in ice-age stone. The rock reader kneels

and flattens his palms: he leans forward,

releases, leans again: how a west-bound

glacier wrote and moved on. To think,

a lexicon left to the elements, meant

for no one's eyes

2.

One step more, we'd drop sky-deep

to the valley below. Where an ice-sheet once

ground south, the breath of summer rises

now, and the Hudson winds like a dragon's

tail gleaming in the sun, no end in sight.

Storied valley! If an artist were to paint

us on this crag, how small we'd seem.

3.

Our feet scuff wanderers' names dated

a century ago. Bold letters that still look

new. Imagine "Li Po" chiseled here,

outlasting my white hair! The rock reader
points north across the river where clouds
skim hills once high as the Himalayas.
I bow, and bow again.

In Between

Michael Lutomski

Standing on a bridge that
dips when trucks roll past
I watch vultures reel
over the river in slow motion
late sun so low on the horizon
it seems like it's standing next to me
the silver of their wings catches
the light and throws it back

I wonder if they ever envy
the legged ones of earth
to arrive without the burn
of the wind and the
biting cold of such heights
could be considered a gift
the same way dolphins
must look at the land
and ponder the true nature
of gravity and the brineless
air that they carry with them
one gasp at a time to the
secret bottoms of the world

I remain a legged one
vultures above
dolphins below
considering the miles
and miles in between

I pitch my cigarette butt
into the river and hope
part of me is stained in the filter
so that the waters can
carry it to the sea

Rose Petals Falling in the Grand Canyon: Wallkill River View

Jan Zlotnik Schmidt

There is a blue quiet
that takes me home
to the stillness of the world

to the dip of a white heron's wing
the slight crackle of
gold aspen leaves in a breeze

the languid lapping
of a turtle's webbed feet
underwater

The only sign
bubbles of breath
concentric circles
on the surface of the pond

This is the gift
the Earth gives

The beating of a stilled heart
A body pulling out of itself

Hieroglyphs
from an unknown scroll

Rose petals
falling in
the grand canyon

Painting

Lynne Digby

Standing behind their easels some paint the view from Boscobel.

Looking down from the rose gardens they see the tidal

waters of Constitution Marsh, rising and falling—rising and falling,

locked in harmony with the moon.

Beautiful river, wide and generous with steep wooded banks,

your waters hide secret faults cracked deep into the Earth's crust.

And your Indian ghosts trek silently along the trails beside,

 "the river that flows both ways."

PART II MEMOIR and ESSAY

The Hudson

Odessa Elliott

For 52 years, the Hudson River has been part of my life. I have driven over it on eight bridges from the Verazzano to Albany; and I've driven beside on highways and local streets in New York and New Jersey. I have taken the Staten Island and NY Waterways across it; and the Lincoln, Holland, and PATH tunnels under it. I have taken trains up both the east and west banks, and I've often flown over it.

My husband loved the river as much as I do. One evening, he decided to go to Weehauken to look at the river and Manhattan Island on a night when the moon made the surface of the water look like polished ebony wood. A little before midnight one New Year's Eve we drove down the West Side Highway with no other cars heading south. In Times Square, the ball was about to drop, but beside the river, there was only snow flakes lazily falling – and silence.

In the early spring, we would drive up the Palisades to the Perkins Tower above Bear Mountain. From there, one can see downstream to the harbor, and upstream past West Point. For several years, there were two decommissioned WWII ships, filled with grain, anchored off the wetlands in Bear Mountain Park. The US later sold the grain to the USSR and towed the barges down to a pier where they were chained to Soviet cargo ships.

One morning, on a Waterway Ferry headed from Hoboken to the marina at the foot of The World Financial Center, I looked out of the window beside my seat and saw an iceberg. Normally, one does not expect to see icebergs that far south on the Hudson, and when I looked across the aisle, I saw more of them. "Is this how the passengers on the Titanic felt?" I wondered. Eventually, I figured out that Manhattan Sanitation workers had cleared snow from the recent record storm and dumped the snow into the river. The air and water temperatures were so low that the snow did not melt. It would disappear, I decided, when it reached the salt water of the harbor. The next morning, however, I decided to play it safe and take PATH to the World Trade Center.

I was at work on the day of the car bomb in the WTC garage. When I heard the explosion, I said to the person to whom I was speaking on the telephone, "That's strange! We usually don't get thunderstorms at this time of the year." Our office receptionist had her radio on and called out out to me: "Just heard the explosion knocked out PATH." I grabbed my purse and coat and headed for the door, announcing: "Gotta get to the ferry before everybody else does!" On my way to the ferry, I was joined by hundreds of persons who'd walked down from the both towers. I had a ticket, so I got out on the second ferry; those without tickets were throwing two dollars in trash cans held by the Waterway staff. I had no idea what had happened, but I suddenly felt very safe to be crossing the Hudson, headed home.

On 9/11/01, my husband had just paid his toll before going up to the ramp to the George Washington Bridge, when he heard on the radio that the GW had been closed because planes had crashed into the Twin Towers. He did a U-turn, and took the Palisades Parkway back north. He stopped at the Rockefeller Lookout, from which one can see all the way to the Harbor, and saw the smoke coming from both towers. Luckily, he got to the Tappan Zee Bridge before it was closed, and wound his way to the Bronx River Parkway and then down local streets to his church office in the South Bronx. I had retired in 1999, and it was several months later before I could get up the courage to take the commuter train to Hoboken to look across the river to where the Towers had stood. I realized the flight to the ferry in 1993 had been a "dress rehearsal" for the massive evacuation on 9/11. Several thousand of those persons headed to the ferries and, just as I once had, felt safe heading home across the river.

Center Stage: Revolutionary African Combatants in the Hudson River Valley (from the book Long Hammering)

Dr. A. J. Williams-Myers

Although marginal, if evident at all, Africans as combatants among European troops were evident from the very inception of Dutch and British colonial rule in New York. That image was captured and written into the records as early as the French and Indian War by a white soldier in a letter to his cousin in Philadelphia after a fierce fire-fight up at Lake George. In the letter the soldier wrote: "the Blacks fought more valiantly than the Whites" – a fact of history forgotten and unsung.

The presence and heroism of America's unsung African combatants was there from the very beginning of the revolutionary conflict, at the battles of Lexington and Concord and even at the Boston Massacre of 1770. It was the presence of Africans, distributed throughout the forces of the Continental lines, state levies, and militias, as with previous wars, who were to turn the tide of war in favor of the Americans. Washington, in the winter of 1777-78 while on the verge of defeat, made the African American presence as a combatant – free and enslaved – official. It was done as well because of the need to ensure a sustained fighting force of 35,000 at all times on the battlefield, even though unofficially such a presence had always been there. For one, when Ethan Allen and his Green Mountain Boys, accompanied by Benedict Arnold, made their dash to the northern slopes of the valley in the region of Lake Champlain in order to capture Fort Ticonderoga and Crown Point in 1775 (subsequently turned over to the command of the Northern Army under General Schuyler), African American warriors were among the regimental units. Later that year, when Arnold dashed through the woods of Maine to rendezvous with the New York regiment of General George Clinton and General Montgomery to join in their disastrous invasion of Quebec City, many young African descendant combatants were there, attached to various Ulster County regiments and from mid-Hudson towns such as

Kingston, Marbletown, and New Windsor.

An important strategic objective of the American forces was to hold the Hudson Valley against British attempts to cut a wedge between the New England states and others farther south. The job of insuring valley security fell to the forces of the Northern Army (first under General Philip Schuyler and later under General Horatio Gates) and to those of the Valley command (under Major-General William Heath and others). Integrated among the forces were African Americans from the valley, many from regiments in New England and New Jersey, and from various southern regimental units.

To help shore up the American's position in this war theater, African Americans assumed an array of roles in addition to combatants. They were drivers, orderlies, waiters, cooks, bakers (especially at Tarrytown, Continental Village, and at Fishkill where there were numerous ovens for baking bread), skilled craftsmen, and common laborers. Many were also engaged at New Windsor on the "works," a point on the Hudson River where the huge iron chain, manufactured with enslaved labor at the Sterling Iron Works in Orange County, was assembled in sections and floated down to West Point. There, sometime after 1777, its five hundred yards was assembled and stretched across the Hudson to Constitutional Island in order to prevent British ships from ascending the river.

Black combatants of the First and Second Regiments of Rhode Island repeatedly demonstrated their military prowess. Under the command of Colonel Christopher Greene, the First Regiment held the British guerrilla group, the "Cowboys," at bay in the Neutral Zone, a region of the lower Hudson Valley which stretched across the extent of southern Westchester County into parts of eastern New Jersey. It was a zone in which those few brave families who elected to remain had to contend with theft, murder, and destruction by renegades, such as the "Cowboys" and "Skinners," who cloaked their plundering under an alleged allegiance to either the British or Americans. Major-General Heath ordered Colonel Greene and his black regiment (First Rhode Island) into the Zone to hold Pines Bridge on the Croton River against the marauding "Cowboys," who fre-quently made incursions from their base at Morrisiania (South Bronx) under the com-mand of Colonel James

Delancey. In an early morning raid on 14 May 1781, Delancey and his "Cowboys" caught Greene and his command by surprise and overran the Pines Bridge post at the Davenport House, killing Colonel Greene, another officer, and many of the Black troops. The Black troops "defended their beloved Col. Greene so well that it was only over their dead bodies that the enemy reached and murdered him."

In the face of such valor and heroism, Americans were assured of ultimate victory. Benedict Arnold and Major John Andre met their Waterloo when their mission to secretly pass the plans to West Point on to the British was foiled by the African American sentry James Peterson of Cortlandt in Westchester. Andre was hanged in October of 1780. With the assistance of the enslaved, Pompey Lamb, General "Mad" Anthony Wayne and his forces were able to capture the British fort of Stony Point on 16 July 1779. Earlier in 1777, the decisive year the French entered the war in support of the Americans, that same valor and heroism was instrumental in the defeat of General St. Ledger's forces in the Mohawk Valley, the eventual repulse in that same year of General Henry Clinton's flotilla back down the Hudson, though his forces did burn Kingston, and finally there was that decisive battle of Saratoga where General Burgoyne surrendered to General Gates. Subsequent to Clinton's failed attempt to link up with St. Ledger and Burgoyne, the huge chain was stretched across the Hudson at West Point.

As General Washington and his French allies bivouacked at White Plains in pre-parations to cross the Hudson River from Verplanck Point at King's Ferry on their way south to confront Cornwallis at Yorktown in Virginia, two eyewitness accounts support that African American presence among the troops. While at White Plains with his French contingent, Baron Ludwig Von Closen remarked that "a quarter of them [American fight-ers] were Negroes, merry, confident, and sturdy." General Rochambeau's aide, Jean-Baptiste-Antoine de Verger, the other eyewitness, observed that day in July 1781:

The whole effect was rather good. Their arms were in good conditions; some regiments had white cotton uniforms. Their clothing consisted of a coat, jacket, vest, and trousers of white cloth, buttoned from the bottom to the calves, like gaiters. Several battalions wore little black caps, with white plumes. Only General Washington's mounted guard and Sheldon's legion [included among both were African Americans] wore large caps with bearskin fastenings as crests. Three-quarters of the Rhode Island regiments consists of Negroes, and that regiment is the most neatly dressed, the best under arms, and the most precise in its maneuvers.

The Hudson River Swim

Barbara Freer

My first experience with the Hudson River was when I was eighteen and moved to Esopus. A pleasant ten minute walk took me past apple orchards to the river where a small dock was situated near the water's edge for small boats or swimmers. Soon I had new friends who frequented the dock in warmer months and swam or cooled off at this spot. It was our gathering place, a social place for us to share laughter, conversations, and fun. We never swam far from the dock for there was no lifeguard or anyone to save us in case of trouble.

Watching the traffic on the river while sitting on the dock was a interesting and relaxing experience often shared with someone. It took us away from homework or other work, and worries flew into the deep of the water as the sun browned our faces, and left us with nothing but joy and a refreshed mood. This was when I was in my teens and still in school.

I moved from Esopus to Port Ewen when I was out of school. There I walked with friends on the River Road where one friend lived. Her father was a shad fisherman and his house was across from the river. Often we watched it from this spot, as we talked.

After I married I saw the Hudson River occasionally and forgot the pleasure of it, swimming in a lake instead. Then one day my cousin, Rosemarie, asked if my husband, Bud, and I wanted to take a ride on her boat on the Hudson. "Sure, we would love it." I responded.

"My dad is coming and bringing some food to cook," she said. "We'll stop someplace to have a barbecue."

"It sounds great," I said. "I'll bring some salad."

"Wear you bathing suit. We usually go swimming off the boat."

On a sunny warm Sunday we boarded the small boat as Rosemarie steered the boat towards the Esopus area. It was great to be on the Hudson again after a long absence of so many years. All was going fine, and in the vicinity of Esopus Island my cousin dropped the anchor, at first having problems, but eventually getting everything right. My uncle threw a large thick rope towards the back of the boat onto which he held and swam. Rosemarie did the same. My husband and I watched. It looked like fun. After a while the uncle and cousin descended from the side of the boat where it was shallow enough to take the picnic supplies onto the island. Bud was still onboard and paid no attention to me as I grabbed the rope and hung on to it in the water. Then I let go of the rope thinking I don't need to hold on a rope; I'm a good swimmer. No one was watching me at that moment as I was trying to swim back to the boat; no matter how hard I tried it was impossible. I couldn't understand it at first and then noticed that the current in the Hudson River kept me from going back that way. Then I swam toward the island. It worked, but for a short time I sure was worried, not being aware of what effect a current can have. I had forgotten, since it was about forty years since I last swam in the Hudson River. It was like the river gave me a little tug saying, "Remember me?"

Ring Of Fire

Werner Hengst

It is a hot, dry afternoon in August, and I am bushwhacking up a steep slope on the southern flank of Bear Mountain. Every few minutes, I stop and sniff the air, testing it for a hint of smoke. So far, there is nothing but the brittle smell of dry leaves, warmed by the sun and stirred up by my sneakers. But I know it's up there, the column of blue-gray smoke I had seen from across the river.

Like many people, I am fascinated by the large, violent spectacles of man or nature. Pictures of tidal waves, explosions or erupting volcanoes are sure to catch my attention. I have never seen a forest fire close up, so I am eager and curious to witness one first hand. Years ago, I had been captivated by the fires that had scorched the sides of Dunderberg, a mountain directly across the Hudson River from Peekskill. In daylight, the whole mountain had been shrouded in smoke, but at night the smoke had been illuminated to an eerie glow from within. It was, in the words of a newspaper article, like looking into the bowels of hell. And who could forget the televised images of the terrible crown fires on the West Coast? Great tongues of flame leaping from treetop to treetop, fanned into a blowtorch by the powerful Santa Ana winds. Not for a minute do I expect to see that kind of conflagration on Bear Mountain. The lack of wind alone would prevent it. But I have done enough hiking on the mountain to know that there is lots of dried-out underbrush. A fire, once started, could quickly spread over hundreds of acres.

After a few more minutes of climbing, I detect a faint burning odor. It's not sharp and unpleasant like the queasy stink of a burnt-out house. Instead, it reminds me of the fall leaves I used to rake into huge piles as a teen-ager, to burn gleefully, with a delicious sense of barely controlled violence. Close to my quarry now, I scramble a few hundred feet further up. The news reports of big forest fires always keep a tally of how many houses and other structures have been lost and whether people have been injured. They never talk about the wildlife. As I follow my nose upwards, I think of all the warblers, garter snakes, squirrels and chipmunks who will be killed or made homeless by even a small fire. Somehow, my empathy does not extend to insects. Having suffered through four episodes of tick-borne disease, I kind of like the idea of roasting deer ticks.

Now, through the underbrush, I see the flames, as yet only a foot or so high. The fire has scorched a level area perhaps a hundred feet across. What's burning is dry leaves and an occasional dry bush or a branch that has fallen off a tree. But the leaves are burning hot and bright yellow, each one's heat igniting those around it. Slowly, the fire front is advancing in all directions. It forms a ring of fire, and a Johnny Cash song by that title starts playing in my head. But where are the firefighters? I expect to see men with hoses and water tanks. But there is no one, not a single person, only me.

What should I do? Obviously, no one has reported the fire to the park office, and it would take me at least half an hour to get there. By the time any kind of firefighting outfit could make it up the mountain, the blaze would be huge. Tentatively, I pick up a fallen branch with a hockey-stick curve at its end and sweep away some of the leaves in front of the fire line. I'm amazed how easily this exposes a tabletop's worth of bare earth and interrupts the flames. So I decide to give it a try. A big clump of dry brush is only a few feet outside the ring of fire. If it ignites, the blaze will escalate quickly, out of control. To stop it, I will have to clear a firebreak at least three feet wide all around the burning leaves, and I will have to work fast.

I start in the most critical spot, near the dry brush. Frantically at first, then with a confident rhythm, I sweep and scrape, sweep and scrape. Johnny Cash, his voice just slightly off-key, sets the beat:

> And it burns, burns, burns
> The ring of fire,
> The ring of fire.

My makeshift tool works remarkably well. But several times, sparks jump my swept area, starting small new fires of their own. I keep having to run back and forth to deal with them. It's like trying to herd cockroaches. I'm beginning to wonder: will I be able to put this thing out, or will it get away from me? If it does, I will have to report it to the park office, maybe even admit my foolish self-confidence, my hubris that served only to delay the *real* firefighters.

But I persist. It is hard and dirty work. I keep sweeping the burning leaves toward the center of the ring where they flare up harmlessly. Slowly, I realize that I'm gaining the upper hand. When I finally work my way around to where I started, the fire is contained. What had been a ring of fire is now just a blackened patch of forest floor. Only some cleaning-up is needed. I walk across the ashes to put out some embers that are still glowing. I don't want their sparks to start another blaze. I stomp on them, I dig up handfuls of dirt to smother them. I actually pee on a couple of stubborn ones. Take that! Smokey the Bear would be proud of me.

I spend a few minutes crisscrossing the area, trying to learn how the fire got started. I expect to find a carelessly abandoned campfire, or some other human cause. But I see nothing. Forensic experts would probably do better. But I am tired, covered with soot and very thirsty. My sneakers, formerly black and white, are a solid black and my feet feel uncomfortably hot. I walk the perimeter one last time, sweeping a long look over the scene from which only a few faint wisps of smoke are rising. Then I scramble back down the mountain to my car, with Johnny Cash still singing in my head.

Maverick Memories

Anthony Robinson

My father first visited the Maverick Art Colony in Woodstock, New York, in 1925. On that visit he met Hervey White, who had founded the Colony twenty years earlier, and he invited my father, a poet and writer, to make the Art Colony his home. In the fall of 1926, with his wife of two days (my future mother), Henry Morton Robinson came to the Colony to live among other poets and painters, sculptors and musicians. The houses were small—no plumbing, no running water. Rent: $50 a year.

Two daughters arrived in quick order. Needing more space for their growing family, my parents bought a farmhouse on Maverick Road immediately across the Art Colony line. It was the house I grew up in. When I was seven my father asked permission from Hervey to turn a scrubby piece of Art Colony land that abutted our property into a field where his son and other Maverick kids (and artists so-inclined) could play ball. Hervey agreed. No cash, no deed exchanged hands. When anthills were leveled and brush cleared, my father hand-painted a sign and nailed it to the locust tree where the two properties met. The sign read: "Hervey's Field." Let the games begin...

Hervey's Field lay in the shadow of a 15-foot-high rearing horse that Maverick sculptor John Flannagan had hewn with an ax from a live chestnut tree. Every day of my young life I saw the Maverick Horse, its head darkened by rain or capped with snow. It represented all that Hervey believed in: freedom and independence for those who made art their calling and wanted a place to live and work.

Different sounds came from the houses in the Colony: the chip-chip of mallet and chisel, the strains of a violin or cello, the voice of an actor practicing lines, the "silence" of a poet or painter. Afternoons and evening, artists gathered at Intelligentsia, a screened-in restaurant, for food and wine, to discuss their work, politics, the world scene. On summer Sunday afternoons in the

Concert Hall, whose rounded roof reminded me of the hull of a great ship, accomplished musicians performed. People came from Woodstock and far beyond to attend; but you didn't have to go in (buy a fifty-cent ticket) to enjoy the music. You could sit or lie in the surrounding woods and fields. Occasionally on Saturday nights the benches would be cleared away for square dancing. How the floor would sink and sag to the dancers' stomping feet, mine among them. A stone's throw from the Concert Hall stood the Maverick Theater; built entirely of raw lumber with pine-slab siding, it sat on a gentle hillside that gave the rear benches higher elevation than those in front. Opening nights were very exciting—the lights, the crowd, the plays. At a time of great hardship in the country, in the depths of a depression, life in the Maverick Colony flourished.

Hervey was growing old. The last house he lived in was an eight-by-ten cabin in a wooded area with a view of the Maverick Horse: a couple of rustic chairs out front, a stone fireplace for cooking. Often I'd sit with him and we would talk about everyday things—trees and animals and weather, the way the sky looked at any one time, why some birds went south and others stayed on. One September day in 1944 I asked Hervey when the leaves first started to fall—a boy's question, as if there were such a day. He gave it serious thought, however, then said, "October 20th." I remember waking on that morning and looking out my window. Of course, leaves had fallen from Maverick oaks and maples the day before and the day before that as well. But on this day the air seemed especially filled with falling leaves. They were everywhere blowing in the wind. It was the day Hervey White died.

As a boy, I wanted the Maverick Art Colony to last forever. But Pearl Harbor came along and everything changed. The artists' houses became empty; Intelligentsia closed; the Maverick Theater lowered its curtain. Certainly, I reasoned, it would all start up again, come back once the war was over. It never happened. Happily, summer concerts continue to this day, a reminder of an era, a time that made an indelible impression on my life. To one side of the Concert Hall stage, protected at long last from the elements, stands the Maverick Horse.

My Hudson River

Judy Mage

I leaned against the top deck railing of the *Hudson River Day Liner* and thought about leaping into the river far below. We were returning to NYC after a month on a farm in High Falls, Ulster County. WWII had ended just weeks earlier. I was ten years old.

Gauging the distance from ship to shore, I wondered if my weak dog paddle could carry me that far. The height of the plunge scared me; could I hold my breath long enough to pop up to the surface? I went down to the lowest deck. Suicide was not in my plans: I only wanted to get back to Pup, the stray dog I'd adopted but been forced to leave behind.

We'd boarded the *Peter Stuyvesant* in Kingston for the trip home. My parents did not own a car, and we took the *Day Liner* each summer to get to "the country" as we in the Bronx called it. I loved those trips north on the river. When we docked at port towns like Nyack, Peekskill, Newburgh and Poughkeepsie, we could watch the teenage boys dive from the pier for coins. The passengers would wrap the coins tightly in strips of paper to slow their descent through the water. How exciting when a boy broke the surface in triumph, holding the tiny package aloft!

Meanwhile, the *Peter Stuyvesant* was sailing further and further away from High Falls. How I would get there after I reached shore, and how I would manage once I got back to Pup were not issues with which I was prepared to deal. We were past Poughkeepsie now, nearing Beacon. I considered trying to get off at one of the ports, but they were only taking on new passengers, and I would surely have been spotted. I decided to wait till the river got narrower, which I remembered was somewhere south of Newburgh.

From where I stood on the lowest deck, the river was just a few yards below, not far to jump. But the swirling waters churned up by the swiftly moving ship were all too visible. I looked back at the huge paddlewheel. Would I have enough time to swim clear before it sucked me down?

I moved as far forward in the boat as I could, and waited, preparing to leap with all my strength.

We were passing the narrow section between the Hudson Highlands and Storm King on the western shore. This was my chance. The huge, dark, looming rock had always enchanted me. But now I hesitated. How would I get over it? I knew nothing about trails that might lead me around the mountain. My fear of getting hopelessly lost combined with my trepidation about those churning, menacing waters as the ship sped along drained away my resolve.

By the time we docked at Cold Spring I knew I'd been defeated. Why hadn't I run away with Pup when I had the chance? I was a coward. I'd betrayed the creature who trusted me, who followed me everywhere, for whom I'd carefully hidden portions of each meal in my napkin, in the dining room of Hoppe's farm boarding house. My parents were not dog people. I'd wept and pleaded in vain for permission to take my beloved pet home to our apartment in the Bronx.

The remainder of the trip down river passed in a fog of misery and self-recrimination.

More than half a century later I am living in New Paltz, having been lured out of Manhattan in 1970 by a fellow member of my volunteer crew on the sloop *Clearwater*. So in a real way, the river brought me here.

Now I am giving something back. I volunteer with Breakfree, an outdoor club at Poughkeepsie High School founded by a retired teacher, an Adirondack Mountain Club leader. I'm in charge of canoe-camping weekends. I teach canoe basics in April and May on a quiet steam and we culminate with a river trip. We have camped off Staatsburg, on Esopus Island, and on the Middle Ground flats north of Hudson. I love these wonderful adventures as much as the kids do.

Now we are camped on a peninsula in a park just north of Cold Spring, and paddling in the Constitution marsh. The fierce wind of the previous day has dropped; the river is a mirror.

My bow paddler, Maria, is 16 years old. She speaks very little English. Recently arrived from Mexico, this is her first Breakfree trip.

I watch her gaze up at Storm King. She's stopped paddling. The mountain is reflected in the silvery surface of the river. Softly, almost to herself, I hear her breathe "*La montaña...qué hermosa!*" My mind flashes on that moment long ago when I sagged against the rail of the *Hudson River Dayliner*, miserable and discouraged, as we passed Storm King and I failed to jump. Now it is so good to be alive, here, on my beloved Hudson River, watching another person fall under its spell.

Family Album

Howard Winn

When I was eight, my father took me on many Sunday mornings not to church but to the New York Central Railroad Station in Poughkeepsie to watch trains storm through or stop. We stood together on a crosswalk above heat and cinders, sometimes caught in the higher eddies of fading steam, and we shared *Good and Plenty*, licorice flavored candy at five cents a box bought at the newsstand inside. Although I have not thought of these moments in a long time, they have meaning. At eight, my daughter skips rope expertly on her toes in my father's living room, having learned lately the game's timing. She leaps just before the ankle tangling sweep of rope swishes below her soles, saying, " I can do something you can't do," to my father at eighty-one. Challenged, he says, "I can do something you can't do." Head down upon the oriental rug, hands complete the triangle as legs erect upwards; soles toward the heaven of his home's ceiling. He does it.

The way it is, my father naps in the middle of every morning; my mother turns off her hearing aid and sleeps every day after lunch. Each watches over the other, not speaking of the inevitable time alone. I remember them running down a beach to the edge of water where he splashed while she shrieked and giggled. I made sand castles.

Thin and dry as goldenrod in December, now he does not remember yesterday, although he knows my name. He says carefully, "Is this the place where I live?" but he goes outside and trims hedges that have obscured windows, leaving doors open by his departure. Found by his wife, he returns, white hair ruffled by ancient breeze, to sit without movement in the same chair that he left. His eyes watch trees from misted panes. Fingers feel smoothed wood. In this moment, he does not turn or speak, but waits as I know him. The worm is in the rose; the flower will not last and is almost true. In his final spring, my father would not let daffodils die a natural death, wilting over green leaves ringing the house, until the trumpets turned brown. He plucked them all in perfection to fill his rooms, yellow and white in every corner.

Stiff in glasses, blooms stood on tables and shelves. Vases holding crisp stems and nodding flowers were whisked away at first signs of decay, replaced by newly opening jonquils in profusion. The faint odor of a single flower multiplied to perfume, bringing April indoors. Empty leaves, stiff as swords, stood about edges of lawn and woods. Even they were gone by the November of his death.

When I last saw him, I was alive. His skin was carefully arranged against the one suit that nearly fit, tailored for this occasion by the embalmer; and he was wearing shoes, tied as he could not tie them. We stood, my mother between my sister and me. We exchanged looks over her head, as she searched for her husband. Perhaps his hand would clench, or his forehead wrinkle, or his pale blue eyes would open while his voice would say, "Don't be foolish, Ruth." He always expected water to part if he needed to cross and she would follow, retrieving whatever fell away from the bundles stacked about his person. He wanted the best. Hart, Schaffner and Marx, Stetson, and not just *for* himself, but within himself. Stromberg-Carlson. Abercrombie and Fitch. Packard. Oldsmobile. His wife. His children. His grandchildren.

The house will not disappear as will not the yard, grass, weeds, chimney, shingles, siding, paint, windows, furnace, faucets, chairs. My father has been dead seven months. His clothes fill the closets, hanging over shoes arranged in rows. His mackinaw remains a presence of plaid in the hall. We all prefer happy endings under a perfectly ordinary sky where the moon can be seen as paler shape in our pale daylight.

The fading photograph is of my father taken during World War I. He stands on a fence post in Texas, as far as he will get from the mighty Hudson River, poised like a ballerina, no support but his two closely placed feet and outstretched arms, holding to hot San Antonio air. His hair is black and full, combed back in pompadour but clipped high on the sides, exposing all of his white ears to sun and wind. Twenty-seven years old, his body is slight and trim, compact in khaki knickers with calves bound by puttees from ankle to knee, but airy as any bird holding to limb or wire, ready for flight.

My father is forever on that post, wild eye observing anonymous camera. My son lures finches in yellow, black or brown behind my eyes in permanent joy. I stand between them always, saying good-bye to my father, who does not go in going, applauding my son who performs unendingly these feats of discipline to capture fantastic flights of real birds. I hold it all here for as long as I am.

Tashlikh-On-Hudson

Amelia B. Winkler

So many images come to mind when I think of the Hudson – the Palisades where I dug for rocks in a Barnard College geology class, the park where we fed squirrels and pigeons, the hill down which my father took my brother and me sleigh riding …

But my strongest memory of "The River" was as a young child in the 1930's and 40's throwing bread and cracker crumbs in the Jewish ceremony of *tashlikh* (Hebrew for "throw"), that symbolical casting of one's sins upon the waters during the High Holy Day period of Rosh Hashanah. Dressed in our holiday best, in my case, a new dress or plaid wool suit and shiny Mary Jane patent leather shoes, we walked as a family, mother, father, son and daughter, to the Hudson River Day Line docks near 125th Street and Riverside Drive and shook our pockets clean. According to Rabbi Joseph Telushkin in *Jewish Literacy,* the custom arose during the Middle Ages and is derived from a verse from the prophet Micah, "And You [God] shall throw their sins into the depths of the sea" (7:19). I'm sure old Peter Stuyvesant would have been turning in his grave if he could have seen us, descendents of the Tribe he didn't want on these shores!

My family would return to the same Day Line docks to take a Day Liner boat up to Indian Point to celebrate my birthday, picnic style. My father's sisters, Rose and Eve, wearing straw hats and gloves, and Eve's cigar-smoking husband were aboard, along with my brother and mother and father and a few family friends. Baskets of chicken and potato salad and thermoses of lemonade were toted, as well as a birthday cake and candles and a blanket to spread for the feast along the river's banks. As a special treat, my brother and I bought Indian headdresses and balloons at the small concession stand. Who could have imagined that a nuclear power plant would be built where we once partied and played?

They say you can't go home again, and while I wouldn't want to return to the very neighborhood I grew up in down by the riverside – Morningside Heights, with its clutch of prestigious institutions: Columbia University, Barnard College, Riverside Church and Grant's Tomb, Juilliard and the Jewish and Union Theological Seminaries–I would love to live some day with a view of the water, but I'm now content with visiting the homes of fellow writers with river views in Tarrytown and Croton and Ossining. But frankly, since dreaming is no sin, I find myself thinking often of the classic "6 rms riv vu". I know I'll find it somewhere, someday, somehow!

Westward Crossing

Penny A. Freel

Early morning rush hour traffic. I am on the Mid-Hudson Bridge, clenching my teeth. Orange poles between the yellow lines divide left and right by a miniscule hand span. I crack the window open to let in a frigid hair of air as the local radio station fades in and out with the report of early morning traffic snarls. I am in a snarl; it is bumper to bumper, decidedly worse going the opposite way, even though I see a patrol car's flashing lights at the end of the bridge on my side. A crawl is better than a full stop. I am heading away from Route 9, away from Poughkeepsie. I am heading west.

I am particularly sensitive to signs. The white van in front of me has big loopy writing scribbled onto its dirty backside door: *Wash me please!* Its back fender sports a faded, jagged white bumper sticker with blue letters, *Jim y ives*: I translate: Jimmy lives, and wonder if it is homage to Jimmy Hendrix. I spot another familiar sign posted on the steel girder nearby the emergency phone: *Your life is worth saving.* Living and dying. Primary concerns for people crossing bridges. A driver lets loose with staccato honks of the horn. Here I am stuck in the middle, still in lockjaw position, jabbing at the off button of the radio, when my dad, James M. or Jim(my) M. to his friends and family, pays me a visit.

Childhood Sunday afternoons were not meant for staying in and watching television. Sunday afternoons meant staying in church clothes and usually going off in the car to visit my dad's brothers and sisters, aunts and uncles, or too many to count cousins who lived in Poughkeepsie. Sometimes though, with a resolute air, my father would herd us into our gray Rambler and take Titusville Road to Route 55 until it became Main Street, then we would make our way past the familiar storefronts and landmarks that made up the city: past Howard Johnson's and Holy Trinity, past Effron's and Woolworth's, Luckey Platt's and Wallace's, past Schwartz's and Mary Abdoo's to travel across the Hudson. No seat belts held us down, so we would clamor against the back of the front seat or, if the weather allowed, we would crank open the windows and hang our heads out so to better our vantage point to win the contest, who

could spot the bridge's towers first. It was more than a game. The
bridge sighting was deliverance from too many Sunday afternoons
spent in stuffy rooms minding manners and listening to noisy
clucking. As we rolled down Main Street, my father would begin
to relax, his fingers tapping out a song on the wheel. My mother,
holding my baby brother, would let out a hefty sigh and a hint of a
smile would play across her face. And then . . . and then the bridge
would loom in the mid-afternoon light, its sturdy hulk waiting
for one and then the rest to yell, *I see the bridge* . . . . Jimmy M.
always lost.

My dad would begin to sing as he maneuvered the car up and
on to the bridge. We, the backseat brigade, were his chorus, for we
were well-versed in Como or Sinatra or a risqué army song. Jimmy
M. would make the crossing at a snail's crawl, so to last a Sunday
afternoon lifetime. The river below watched as my father, our
trailblazer, kept to his steady course and kept his eyes westward,
but every so often, reflected in the rearview mirror, his eyes would
meet ours in expectation and delight. We knew what came next.
Jimmy M. would sound the horn. This was ritual for any bridge
or tunnel or railroad crossing he would come to, but this crossing
always seemed special. Not a gentle honk but a long loud lush
blast announced to the city behind us, to the river below us, to the
train tracks on either side, to the black freight bridge to the right of
us, and to those other escapees that we were on the Mid-Hudson
Bridge, alive and very well, thank-you-ever-so-much. My sisters
and I would plead for one more sounding, but my dad would shake
his head, *uh-uh*, and smile. We would finish the crossing and go
a few miles up or down the other side of the river, stopping in
accordance to the season, for ice cream, a Christmas tree, or to a
farm stand for apples or corn, and then my father would turn the
car around and we would begin our journey back. The westward
process would not be repeated going back home.

Another irate honk from yet another impatient traveler sounds.
The sound moves forward toward me; I am going west, just as
Jimmy M. did on those infrequent Sunday river rides. I do not need
to ride the brakes now, and shift from second into third gear, then
into fourth. I am almost to the other side; my teeth are no longer
clenched. I begin to tap out a tune on the wheel, and just for the
hell of it, press down hard on the horn.

Memoir

Jonathan M. Freiman

I was born in New York City in 1950 on May 30th, Memorial Day. It was easy to think, jokingly as a child, that the parade under our 11th floor apartment on Riverside Drive was in my honor.

The view was wonderful from there. A beautiful verdant expanse called Riverside Park was immediately across the street. It was rich with paths and benches, playgrounds and promenades, and broad stairways down to a walkway by the Hudson itself. Beyond the western bank of the river towered the New Jersey Palisades.

I had a favorite perch from which to watch the constant activity on the grand boulevard below, the park with cyclists and skaters and hula-hoopers, the West Side Highway traffic, the green-blue swells of the Hudson, and Jersey beyond. It was a sturdy, wooden radiator cover that concealed the old cast iron steamer beneath. It did get quite toasty in winter, abbreviating my observation time, but the rest of the year it proved a fine bench.

At the age of six, I discovered where my father kept his prized binoculars. With those in hand I could zoom in on mothers in the park sunning their babies, dog walkers before the age of the pooper scoop, and any of the ships and barges plying the often choppy waters as they headed up and down river.

Periodically, the Navy would anchor a ship at mid-river. I always hoped for a warship rather than a support vessel. Being properly armed myself with a cap gun on each hip, (fully loaded with 50 shot perforated rolls) I wanted to see a man-of-war with proper armament as well. Sometimes a gray destroyer would pause for a few days. Other times a large cruiser, still wearing the camouflage paint of combat duty, would sojourn there.

I remember springtime that year, looking out from my perch, the radiator comfortably cool, and spying the grandest ship of all. It was surely a battleship! Twin turrets forward with main guns raised, single turret aft, pennants flying, and the rest of the ship bristling with smaller cannons, all fit the description. What joy! My father and mother, brother and grandmother all remarked at its majestic, brooding silhouette. Best of all, it was open to the public for a short time.

We walked down to the 79th Street Boat Basin, and after a short wait, boarded a motor launch the Navy was using to shuttle civilians to and fro. I sat near the stern where the helmsman steered the tiller as the deep burble from the engine's exhaust filled our ears. Up a steep ladder to the deck we carefully climbed. Once there, I remember friendly sailors describing the various parts of the ship and one even lifting me up to see through the massive, pedestal mounted binoculars. I figured aloud these were not the kind you wore around your neck.

After a few days the ship departed with the aid of mighty tugs all about. Fireboats led with a cataract salute. Looking back now I realize we were the inheritors of a hard won Pax Americana that began at the end of the Second World War. The ships I saw were battle-hardened veterans of a ferocious conflict from which America emerged as the only nation with an intact military and industrial base.

Different ships now visit New York Harbor. The dreadnought is a museum. The little boy grew up, and the Hudson still flows out to the sea.

Cowheads

Nancy O. Graham

June 2003

"Is it okay to swim in the Hudson?" I ask a new friend. Henry and me and our kids—Ray is five and Ada three—have moved upriver from the city. Suddenly all our friends are new friends.

"I won't swim in a Superfund site," she answers.

But surely the lifeguards at Kingston Point beach test the water, I figure.

As if in warning, the beach is mined. Spiny nuts the size of a quarter pierce my children's feet. The sand is muddy, the water unnaturally warm, and we step repeatedly on the nuts. I pack up our Band-Aids and dirty towels and promise we'll try another swim area some other day.

What was I thinking—I'd never swim in the East River or the Gowanus Canal, would I?

July 2004

The pool is nut-less but smells like a mop and lacks shade, breeze, a horizon, so we keep exploring the riverscape: Saugerties Light House, Mills Mansion, Sleightsburgh Spit. I know to pick my way to the beach. I've learned a few things about the water chestnuts. They're not the kind in Chinese stir-fry; you can't eat these, they're bad.

If some locals feel sketchy about bathing in the Hudson, the water chestnut doesn't. It thrives and multiplies, hogs oxygen, threatens other water plants and fish, provokes ecologists.

This non-native swimmer is the only one happy about its presence in the river.

I feel for the water chestnut. As a newcomer I'm prickly, distracted, floating on memories of crowded sidewalks, trying too hard and too fast to put down roots. Maybe I'm an invasive species too.

August 2005

Our favorite hiking spot is the Black Creek trail, which leads over
a footbridge and up a thigh-straining hill, winds past vernal pools
and a stone wall, then descends, with promising flashes of white
expanse, toward the river. On banks where tides have chipped
away plates and skipping stones of shale, Ada plays chef. An
oblong slate of sushi appears under my nose. Bark bits rolled in
moss and tied with blades of grass, and water chestnuts that thrust
their tiny lances toward my lips as I pretend to eat one.

"Mmmmm, what a delicacy, better than a sea urchin."

September 2006

At Ulster Landing the swim area is roped so kids won't go in
over their heads. A barge passes, and the lifeguard whistles the
swimmers out of the water to keep the undertow from sucking
them below and away toward the city and the sea.

Children swarm out of the water and bury themselves in wet,
brown sand. Ray rises, staggering, a swamp thing. He'll get sand in
his eyes. I have to go tell him to be careful.

"Ouch! Yah! Dammit!" I step on one of the little nasties.

Stooping to pick it up, I hold it between thumb and forefinger.
The shape—round center sprouting needle-nose tendrils—
resembles a cancer cell. I've read somewhere that cancer rates are
higher among people who live along the Hudson.

"That's a cowhead," says Sara, eight years old, the daughter
of Ulster County natives who have become our good friends. Our
dear friends, I think, admiring Sara's long eyelashes as she looks
down at the water chestnut, now a what? *Cowhead.*

I peer at the nut. Held a certain way, yes, it becomes the head
of a black cow. The scar where it once joined the stem of the plant
makes the base of a snout. Lumps along the periphery suggest ears.
Two horns curve gently but woundingly toward me from the top.

"You call this a cowhead?"

"Sure. Everyone does."

October 2007

Standing in the etymology section of the library—my library, I
have walked to it every week for five years—I notice an oversize
book on medieval weaponry and begin to page through its pen-
and-ink drawings. My eye lands on a ball with four metal points
arrayed, the book tells me, so that one of them always stood
straight up. Flung on a field of battle, they crippled the charging
horse. Caltrops, they were called.

    I research water chestnuts. I want to know what is being done
to discourage them, to make the river healthy and diverse again.
On the Internet I learn they're called water caltrops, the Latin name
being *Trapa natans*. *Trapa*, from the Latin term *calcitrapa*, for that
medieval weapon. *Natans*, from *natare*, to swim, to float.

November 2008

A fall walk along the Hudson shoreline, sunny, fallen leaves still
plump and yellow, beach littered with seaweed and whatnot.

    Ada, now nine, says, "Let's do some beachcombing."

    I crouch to pick through the detritus. A toddler, the age Ada
was when we moved, tells her father she wants to look for shells.

    No shells. Water chestnuts, yes, cowheads, *caltrops*—hundreds
of them—pushed by the tide into a wavy line. I cradle a handful;
their points dig lightly, teasingly into my palm. I clear the beach of
them and take them home in a tin bucket. I take them home.

River Generations

Madeline Mazzetti Labriola

"What do you think is one of the most unique features of the Hudson Valley?" I asked my 8th grade students one day. Their mouths remained shut; they had a dumbfounded look on their faces, and their foreheads wrinkled into that "How am I supposed to know" expression. I was hoping that someone would notice that they lived on the shoreline of the majestic Hudson River, which they could practically see from the classroom window. But nobody did and I wondered why?

Maybe they never sat outside on the deck at Mariner's Harbor on a late summer's night to watch the sunset over the ridge that gives Highland its name. The sky would turn pink and orange and the soft darkness would fall around me as I sat by the water. Surrounded by friends, I was celebrating the birth of my first grandchild. The lobster dinner, although not from the river, helped me have a deep sense of appreciation and gratitude for life's bounty.

I guess my students had never gone for a speed boat ride on a Sunday afternoon, going no place in particular, just up and down the river, just to be on the river with my father and mother and three bratty brothers. Or maybe they never had the good fortune to travel by train to NYC passing all the little river towns along the way and see West Point's gorgeous stone walls, or wonder who lived in that house, or what was the old Bannerman's castle doing standing so stranded in the river? Then they wouldn't know how the mist rises early in the morning along the silver river shore and the ducks and water birds dip and play in the small inlets.

No, my students wouldn't know about the Hudson River Day Line that steamed along from NYC to Highland Landing that brought my grandparents from the city to the country where they were to buy a farm and raise ten children in the midst of a great depression.

And it was sad to think that they didn't know about one of my favorite pastimes in high school called the submarine races. That was when I would disobey my parents and go to the place where the bridge on the Highland side had a parking area that overlooked the river. I could sit and talk for hours with my favorite boyfriend and watch the lights twinkle on the bridge as the black river flowed far below. Maybe we got a kiss or two in before the local police would show up with big flashlights shining through the steamy windows. I never did see a submarine, but at sixteen it didn't seem to matter.

That day I thought, "How did these young people miss seeing the Hudson River, even if it was only from the view from the Mid-Hudson Bridge as they were going shopping at the mall?" At that moment, I knew I had to take drastic measures. These students could not go through their lives without knowing the Hudson River. The next day I signed them up for a trip on the *Clearwater*.

Rivers and Bridges I Have Known

Janet Neipris

Rivers running to the sea, rushing towards oceans, lapping shores, caressing inlets, busy rivers, silent and deep rivers, gentle rivers, rivers of our youth, of our children, of our travels, autumn rivers.

The first time I saw the Hudson River was on a trip from Boston to New York to take my three young daughters to the theater. It was a production of Steven Schwartz's "Pippin," and we drove alongside what I thought was the most magnificent bridge I had ever seen, the George Washington Bridge, the entryway to New York City. We all were strangely silent, in awe, and then burst into—well, you can guess—the song "George Washington Bridge." The GW Bridge is 4,760 feet in length and was built in 1927, crossing the Hudson River at its narrowest point. Made of cable and steel beams which gleam across the sky, the bridge, with its two levels, remains a monument of grace in the cacophony of the city. South of the GW, the river meanders along Riverside Park and the New York skyscrapers on its western side with New Jersey and its town houses and newly constructed apartment buildings on the other, before it empties into New York Harbor and then into the Atlantic where the Statue of Liberty lifts her lamp. The Hudson River, at the place where it is crossed by the George Washington Bridge, marks the spot where you know you are home, if indeed you are coming to live on the island of Manhattan. In New York City, where I lived the majority of my mid-years, the East River does boast of its ten bridges, from the Throgs Neck at its northernmost point to the Brooklyn Bridge at its southernmost point; but, it was always the Hudson for me because of its grandeur and power. When I moved to New York City in the 1980's, little did I know what a major part the Hudson would later play in my life.

I had always dreamed of a house by the ocean. Maybe it's because I'm a Pisces. Maybe it's because water has life and energy and movement. So, when I fell in love with the Hudson

Valley, it was a surprise. But the lure of the sweet farmland and the mountains and the old stone houses and barns shot an arrow through my heart, and when we came across an old farmhouse in Stone Ridge, New York, with a stream running behind its barn, we knew we were home. We would later discover that this stream joined the Rondout Creek, a tributary of the mighty Hudson River.

The Hudson River was discovered by Henry Hudson, the Dutch explorer, while looking for a route to the Pacific in 1609, and he described it as the "River of Mountains," although the Native Americans called it "Muhheakunnuk" meaning "great waters constantly in motion." Hudson also noted in his journals that, "It is as pleasant a land as one can tread upon." Some things don't change. The farmland along the Hudson River Valley remains some of the richest in the country, and boasts the best corn in America as well as apples.

In the years since we bought our house, my life has become closely tied to the Hudson River, but a different river than the one I had first known, running under the George Washington Bridge. This newly discovered Hudson, once I crossed over the Tappan Zee Bridge, which spans the Hudson at its widest, maintains the true grandeur of Henry Hudson's river. It's no surprise that the Hudson Valley painters saw the region as the true picture of "God's America."

There's not a week I don't cross the Kingston-Rhinecliff Bridge, a four lane, half- mile, continuous truss, open-decked bridge, built on the site of the old ferry crossing. This bridge carries more than 20,000 cars a day, and because of the way it's constructed, all the support is under the roadway, so that the view is unobstructed for all its passengers. In all its seasons, and on a sunny day, especially, it is as if you are flying over a magical, shimmering carpet of water. In contrast, the George Washington Bridge, because of its suspension construction, obscures the Hudson River and the sky because of its cables and towers. I cross the Kingston-Rhinecliff Bridge, just twenty minutes from my home, for a multitude of good reasons. It is either to go to the year–round Sunday Farmers Market at Rhinebeck or the local produce stands in summer, to Bard for a performance in the new Frank Gehry designed Fisher Center, or to the romantic Poet's

Walk where Washington Irving and William Cullen Bryant strolled in Red Hook, New York, or to the Clermont, with its panoramic views of the Hudson, owned by Robert Livingstone, co-inventor of the steamboat. Sometimes, it's just to have dinner with friends at Gigi's Cafe on Main Street, then across the street to the Upstate Film Theater to see the latest independent film. But always, it's the promise of seeing the Hudson River which draws us.

The Rip Van Winkle Bridge, NY 23, goes from the Catskill shoreline on the west, to Hudson in the east, famed for its antiques. This cantilevered bridge with its Dutch style tollbooth, is used mainly to visit friends as far away as Germantown, Chatham or Copake, and all the way passing rolling fields of grain and dairy farms which have remained the same longer than Rip Van Winkle lay asleep. And in the autumn, like this autumn, trees as golden as honey on either side. Heaven, home. The Hudson River Valley, where farmers still farm, and on every corner a sign "Support your local growers." And we all do.

This is the Hudson River of Pete Seeger and his sloop, *Clearwater*, of George Washington and his soldiers in the Revolutionary War, the Hudson Valley surrounded by mountain chains, the Catskills and the Shawangunks, home to Presidents and tillers of soil, artists and writers, carpenters and architects, bakers of pies and pie-eyed dreamers. It's my home. This land is my land.

The Hudson

Mary Armao McCarthy

"Do the docks have to go into the river this early?" I ask my husband Kevin. He is bundling up for the April round of male bonding called Docks-In at our upstate New York marina. Kevin just laughs while layering on another shirt and pulling his knee pads and back brace off the closet shelf. His job during Docks-In is Pin Puller. That means he spends the weekend on his hands and knees inserting large metal locking pins to connect 5 X 12 foot wooden docks in a floating pattern that eventually holds seventy boats. A squadron of fellow boat owners and machinery complete the job that provides a season of companionable boating on the Hudson River.

Our part of the river runs from Kingston to Troy, NY, each a lazy day trip on our 26-foot Sea Ray. It's a good old boat on a good old river. The twenty year-old boat came to us five years ago. The river—well, it's been here since the ice ages.

Kevin and I started boating a decade ago by renting canal boats for summer vacations. We regularly met boaters doing "The Big Loop" the circle formed by the Hudson River, Erie Canal, the length of the Mississippi, and the Eastern Seaboard's Intercoastal Waterway. We were surprised how often "Loopers" told us that the Hudson was the most beautiful water they had been on. And so, when Kevin fulfilled his boyhood dream of buying a boat, we put it on the Hudson River.

Beauty and history reside on the banks of the river and come to us over its water. Sometimes we share the river with the *Half Moon,* the colorful replica of Henry Hudson's vessel. Other times we see the *Clearwater,* the reproduction of a graceful 1800's sailing sloop built by folk singer Pete Seeger and friends. Years ago, when Kevin and I took our daughter Christine to see the newly launched *Clearwater*, we were lured by the boat and Pete's banjo, not realizing that he was also catching us as human fish in a net cast to educate the public about the river.

The Hudson is a transportation microcosm. On an afternoon of leisure boating, we can pass ocean going barges while planes fly above. We float under bridges while cars and trucks pass overhead. On each shore, trains glide by like toys in a diorama, freight trains on the west bank and Amtrak passenger trains on the east.

We once boated to Olana, deciding it was a sentimental way to visit the home of the river's famous painter, Frederick Church. We have cruised as far south as West Point, where Revolutionary war soldiers stretched a chain across the water at the foot of stately Storm King Mountain and held back a British invasion. Battles still wage on the river, but now they are over additional commercial ports, water quality, PCBs, cement plants, green space, and even the impact of our 26-foot motor boat. The Hudson River helped launch the modern environmental movement in the 1960's when landmark court cases saved this ecosystem and Storm King Mountain itself from a mega-power plant.

Kevin and I can boat through pastoral countryside, past the ghostly ruins of an abandoned ice house and to such picturesque water towns as Athens and Castleton. Day trips north bring us through the industrial wonders of the Port of Albany and to the upper reaches of the Hudson's tides in Troy. Tides from the Atlantic travel 150 miles north to Troy, where they are stopped not by nature, but by a massive Federal dam and lock. Boating can be challenging on the Hudson River because its constant southerly current combines with the changing direction of the tides. Native Americans call it "the river that runs two ways." Technically, the river is an estuary. Salt water from the Atlantic Ocean flows upstream as far as Poughkeepsie.

We have a tide clock on the wall of our family room at home. It keeps us in touch with the river. The tide clock's single hand marks not time but the level of the tide. Changing tides create a four foot difference in water height where our boat is docked, and a full moon brings a greater difference. It is easiest to leave our mooring at high tide, when the channel is deepest. For Docks-In, when Kevin helps to wrestle the docks into the river, the two hours of slack tide are helpful— that period when the tide stills before reversing direction again. Our marina uses floating docks rather than stationary piers, to avoid constant adjustments to mooring lines as water levels change. There is an hour difference in tide time between our home in Albany and our boat dock. Unvarying in this mix is the cycle of the tides, shifting twice a day from high to low. The dial of our tide clock is mounted on an ornate compass rose design. Its readings are a manmade reminder of the constancy and change of the river.

A Sea Change on the Hudson

Betsy McCully

The *Half Moon* chugs across the water, belching diesel smoke. Braving the fumes, I watch the boat's wake cut a white swath through the blue swell. The American flag mounted on deck snaps in the wind, framing my photo of the Manhattan skyline. I'm on a cruise of the waterfront sponsored by Hidden Harbor Tours. I've done my homework. Having read Robert Boyle's classic *The Hudson: A Natural and Unnatural History*, I know the harbor has 650 miles of navigable shoreline. This was what attracted European explorers four centuries ago.

When Henry Hudson nosed his ship through the Narrows into Upper New York Bay, he would not have known that the harbor was once a lake, nor that a glacier high as the Statue of Liberty surged over Manhattan, sculpting the harbor's bowl. Hudson was bent on his present course: to find the Northwest Passage to the Spice Islands. When he sailed past Manhattan, the waterway narrowing to a ribbon, he thought he had found it. His heart must have quickened as the river unspooled before him, tacking northeast then tacking northwest.

On a map the Hudson is a slightly meandering blue line that treads due north from Manhattan to Albany. If you enlarge the map, you can trace the river's tortuous course as it bends southwest at Hudson Falls and winds through the Adirondacks to its source. That's the visible river, measured at 315 miles from the headwaters to Manhattan's tip. The invisible river is revealed in nautical charts as a deep channel extending through the Narrows another 120 miles to the edge of the continental shelf. During the ice age, when sea level was 350 feet lower than today, a glacier diverted the Hudson from this ancient channel. Draining the waters of the Hackensack, Passaic, and Raritan rivers, the Hudson roared across the exposed shelf and cascaded into the sea, sluicing sediments 160 miles east to the Abyssal Plain. When the glacier receded around 18,000 years ago, its terminal moraine blocked the Hudson's outflow, impounding it. Around 12,000 years ago, the lake breached the moraine at the Narrows, bursting with such force it scoured the gap 200 feet down to bedrock. The river coursed into its ancient channel, its torrential falls carving a 15,000-foot-deep gorge known as the Hudson Canyon.

Today, fishermen know the Hudson's drowned mouth as the Mudhole, populated by fish that thrive in silted bottoms. Boyle tells us the Mudhole was for years the city's dumping ground, where rubble from Manhattan building projects now attracts fish like black sea bass. The Hudson Canyon was first explored by William Beebe of the New York Zoological Society in the 1920s. Beebe trawled up from its frigid depths, "pink treasure, glittering and gleaming, trembling with strange vitality, every spoonful a cosmos of hundreds of living beings." One of the strangest was a fish with a duck-like bill, stalked eyes, and "scores of glowing portholes" lighting its filament-like body. The canyon abounds with extraordinary diversity, harboring species adapted to both cold and warm waters— dragonfish, lancet fish, scarlet shrimp, thousand-pound leatherback turtles, porpoises, dolphins, tuna, bluefish, marlins, swordfish, sharks and whales.

By six thousand years ago, the sea reached its modern level, filling the harbor and creating the New York archipelago. High tides push upriver, and the river flows down, meriting the Lenape name for the Hudson, *Mahicanituk*, "the great waters, or seas, always ebbing or flowing." The mixing of salt and fresh waters makes the Lower Hudson a vast estuary, a geologically rare ecosystem dependent on a stable sea level. River sediments build mud flats where cord grasses take root, forming wetlands. These are nurseries for a multitude of marine animals – oysters, mussels, clams, crabs, fishes – and a host of creatures who feed on them, from birds to humans.

Looking back at Manhattan receding from the boat's wake, I feel the great upheaving swell of the sea, and the pulsing of the ancient river. Like Henry Hudson, most of us are bent on our present purposes, narrowing our focus to the ribbon of our human existence. I could recount centuries of overfishing, wetlands destruction, and pollution in the Lower Hudson – but that sad litany would take pages. What matters now is that we've turned a page in that history as we act to restore the river. This turnaround could not have been possible without a sea change in the way we see the Hudson. Since Verplanck Colvin discovered the Hudson's source in 1872, describing it as "a minute, unpretending tear of the clouds, as it were – a lovely pool shivering in the breeze of mountains," we've begun to see the whole watershed. Colvin's epiphany led to the creation of Adirondack Park, when the concept of "forever wild" was inscribed into law. A century later, Pete Seeger launched the *Clearwater*, and citizens began to reclaim the river from polluters and return it to nature. In all these acts, we recognize the Hudson's ecological value. It's a river of life, always ebbing and flowing.

Poems Paddled Down the Hudson

Pam Mitchell

In death nothing moves, not even the waters of this mighty river. Or does it? I hear the voices of my people moaning in this frozen ice.

Closing my eyes to the sun's warmth, the gentle words of my grandmother soothe me: "What a joy you have been to me" her words inscribed upon the back of her painting of the Hudson River. She passed on, leaving me the river that has carried the dreams of my ancestors. Sailing upstream from New York. Flowing downstream from its headwaters where they settled below Lake Tear of the Clouds.

My people; Adirondack solid; full of the hope that moves life, and rivers, forward.

Shortly after September 11, 2001, that river was to carry a man named Christopher, a retired airline pilot, down its waters. One day while Christopher was perusing the aisles of a kayak store in Albany, he overheard me asking the owner if he knew anyone who might help me with a wild idea. Christopher came forward and offered to help. He agreed to become my accomplice in a plan to feed the rescue workers of New York City with poems of encouragement. Poems tenderly wrapped in a map case, stowed within the hold of his kayak, and paddled down the Hudson.

It was early October in the aftermath of 9/11. I was teaching English at a community college many miles upstream in Glens Falls. The rubble of the Twin Towers was still smoking. I could only imagine the stench. I was also a nurse with an instinct to help. My mind kept returning to the river. It was our connection. Knowing the power of poetry, I envisioned sending students' poems downriver. In addition to poems, I wanted balsam fir needles. I knew their healing qualities. I also knew the generosity of my Adirondack kinfolk. Traveling north following the Hudson,

I veered west into the mountains. Asking my people for balsam, I received a box of 50 small pillows filled with fragrant needles, to be paddled with the poems.

It was cold, late-November-New-York-cold. Christopher was launching his beautiful kayak on the Hudson at the Albany port. My students christened it with water from Adirondack lakes and blessed it with branches of White Pine.

Christopher paddled every day, for one hundred and fifty miles. I was base command, scattering maps on my living room floor, while following his progress.

Once he nearly quit when his dry suit ripped and he feared tipping into the frigid Hudson. Wise pilot that he is, he knew he could quickly die. However, his partner brought him the necessary supplies for repairs. He continued while I made little dots on the map of the river as it snaked its way down to New York.

Christopher checked in, using my cell phone, telling me how cold he was, and how he longed for a hot shower. I began to feel guilt and worry that this man agreed to my plan.

In the looming darkness of Yonkers, Christopher phoned from the river that he was seeing lights. An elderly man appeared, waving an American flag, welcoming him to their yacht club that contained a shower, albeit a cold one. He was welcomed, warmed in blankets and fed. Pulling out his sleeping bag, he dozed on the yacht club floor, only to resume his final approach into New York harbor in the morning.

Meanwhile, I loaded my students of poetry into a van. We arrived early at Pier 33 in Manhattan. Walking across the street to the still-smoking debris of the Twin Towers, we distributed the balsam pillows to the workers. They took them in their hands, sniffed them, and marveled at the scent. They had never smelled balsam and kept asking what else was in them to make them so sweet. Thanking us, they tucked them into breast pockets where the scent was readily available. None of us was prepared for the scale of the damage we witnessed, or the horror of the smell.

Not wanting to miss Christopher's arrival, we walked back across the street, and waited a bit longer. As we watched, a quiet, simple entrance into the New York harbor ensued on that 17th day of November. No press would welcome Christopher as he contemplated the horror endured by his colleagues now dead. However, he was not to enter alone.

The collegiality of kayakers is often a strong bond. It was true that day when five men and one woman from New York quietly paddled upriver to greet the man they had never met, but whom they heard was carrying poems.

As we stood waiting, video camera poised, they suddenly rounded the bend of the river and entered the harbor in V-formation like a flock of wild geese. Raising their paddles above their heads, they began howling in ancient, primal chants that seemed to come from somewhere deep within the river.

I realized this river was no longer frozen in death. Moaning became chants. Disbelief melted and the river had become our Hope.

The River Rats, 1973

Jack Murphy

South of the Port of Albany, the six of us carried our overloaded canoes down to the shore and shoved off, destination Eddyville. It was late May, and we were starting a four-day, three-night trip down the Hudson. The first day was spent getting comfortable in the canoes, developing a paddling rhythm, and trying to feel at ease on the river. We stuck close to the shore for a few miles. As the river widened, we tested our confidence and rowed across to the east bank then back out to the middle. We were ready to meet the challenge of life on the open sea.

With evening approaching and the temperature falling, we picked a deserted island to pitch camp. It rained all night and the temperature was in the thirties. We crowded under our tarp trying to find dry spots, but capillary action turned our sleeping bags into sponges as they sucked the moisture from the sand beneath us. By dawn, with the rain still coming down and everyone cold and soaked, we decided that we couldn't possibly be any worse off back in the boats and on the river. We set off for the nearest town and some hot coffee and breakfast. The rain let up as we rowed, and paddling generated some body heat, so we were actually starting to feel a bit better about everything. Then it started snowing.

Down river, the town of Coxsackie came into view. We landed at a public boat launch just as the snow stopped. The bulkhead screened us from view, so we all stripped out of our wet clothes into something dry, tried to comb our dripping hair and pick the detritus out of our beards, then stowed our gear and dragged the canoes up the boat ramp. The neon of a tiny diner beckoned. There were only a couple of small tables, so we seated ourselves on the beat-up red leather-topped spinning stools at the counter. The cook, who eyed us suspiciously, was the only person in the place. As he poured coffee and passed out the menu, each of us took turns in the bathroom. We washed and brushed our teeth, trying to look presentable. When the last of our crew was finished and seated, we signaled the cook that we were ready to order. He was on the phone, said he'd be with us in a minute, and disappeared into the kitchen. When he came to take our orders, he kept dropping his pencil and looking up towards the door. I guess we looked a lot more ragged and threatening than we thought we did. Maybe he thought we were Charlie Manson followers. He took our orders and quickly disappeared back into his kitchen. We sat there waiting to be fed.

A few minutes later the door opened, and in strode two cops and a guard from the nearby state prison. The cook peeked out around the kitchen wall. He had dropped a dime on us! One mean looking cop blocked the door as the guard and the other cop passed behind us very slowly. The guard eye-balled each of us, then, looking to the cop, shook his head no, and left with the cop who was standing by the door. The remaining cop sat down, grabbed a coffee, then looked over at us and asked "Where you boys from?" Before we could answer, he followed up his first question with "Are them your boats down by the dock, there?" We answered the second question first, and then told him we were from New Paltz, and were on a trip down the river from Albany. "New Paltz," he said, "that explains them hippie hairdos." Waving his thumb back in the direction of the cook, he said, "John here thought you all mighta tunneled outta the prison and were stealin' them canoes to escape. That's why he called me down here. Heck, you all just a bunch a river rats. Were you stuck out in that rain all night? And I'll betcha ya didn't plan for snow in May."

That broke the ice. It turned out he had spent most of his life out on the river doing pretty much what we were doing. He couldn't wait to retire and get back out on the Hudson full-time. He sat with us until we finished eating, reliving his youth in his stories about the river. He walked down to the launch with us, and told us about an island down river with squatters' cabins on it. Said we should camp there that night as there was more rain in the forecast. It occurred to me that the river was like a clubhouse, and anyone with ties to the Hudson was a member of the club. As we got into the canoes and started out into the channel, our new friend was still standing there waving. He had given us some good advice, but he also gave us our name for the rest of the trip, the River Rats.

Hudson River Reminisce

Chelsea Whitaker

I remember years ago, when I was seven or eight, my Grandfather would come up from Florida to visit. He used to live in several towns throughout New York, so when he came to visit, he was reliving memories and creating new ones for me and my sister who was eleven or twelve at the time.

Most of my memories of my Grandfather in New York were even as simple as bringing us to the park or having dessert at Micky's Igloo, a local ice cream parlor. The most significant memory is riding the Rip Van Winkle, a cruise ship that sailed down the Hudson River. The cruise started at the Strand down in Kingston, New York. I remember walking onto that half-blue, half-white colored boat. The boat was huge at the time, filled with strangers, talking happily with each other. No matter who you were, everyone was there for one reason and one reason only – to embrace the beauty of the historic Hudson River Valley. I don't remember the names of sights or even how long the ride was. All I do remember is that experiencing those monuments with my family was one of the best days of my life.

As I grow up to be a sixteen year old girl with her license, I begin to appreciate the beauty that my town has. For years I believed the town was boring and useless. I wanted to live somewhere exciting like New York City or even Los Angeles. They are both great places, but the real beauty for me is sitting down on a bench at the Strand, looking out at the slow rippling water. Adults, children and animals pass by you, taking in the beauty of nature. You even could see numerous boats treading the water on a nice sunny day. Even experiencing the Fourth of July fireworks from the Strand is a breathtaking sight.

Researching and becoming more involved in my town, I drove down a road called River Road in Port Ewen, New York. All the houses on the street overlook the Hudson River. A perfect place to live until the recession started. Thin ice covered the sides of the river, snow particles on top of the ice. Right in the middle of the River, the water still flowed. To prove the point, a barge began to pass in front of me.

The barge brought back memories to a time in my life when my old best friend used to live right on the river. On warm days we'd throw on our bathing suits and life jackets to jump off her dock and swim around. Jumping off the dock usually held most of our day. Running off the dock, falling into the river and then swimming to the rocks where the river was shallow, we repeated the whole process over again. Being children, with unstoppable energy, we still had time for games. After a swim in the river, my friend, her twin sisters, their neighbors and I would get together and play hide and seek ... no place off limits. We'd find people running down on the rocks, the water seeping through their shoes. Some people would even hide in the boat house, where an abandon boat laid. It wasn't until the sun fell completely and we could only see outlines of bodies that my friends' mother finally called us in.

When my driving trip was over one weekend, I found my laptop and quickly googled the Hudson River's Rip Van Winkle cruise route. I was interested in seeing the names of the lighthouses and even some pictures. One of the most interesting facts I found was that the cruise passed by the Dinsmore House, which was once inhabited by a women who had remarried after her husband died in *The Titantic* in 1912. Being a teenager and rewatching the movie, *The Titantic,* only weeks before, I became very interested. *The Titantic* was one of my favorite topics to learn about. Hearing about the Dinsmore makes me want to take the cruise ship over again this spring or summer.

Unfortunately, I know the experience will never be the same without my grandfather as he is too weak to think about taking a trip here to New York. I do hope that whether I live my life here in Kingston, New York or somewhere else in New York, that I will relive these memories with my children and grandchildren at some point in my life. I believe it is important to show the people you love the place you grew up as well as the history behind the town and the River. The children don't appreciate the beauty at first, but in the long run with each year, they'll realize the importance of what you've taught them.

It's all about the memories.

My River

Linda J. Still

My mother, Jean Flora Devoe Casey, spent her girlhood *in* or *on* or *near* the Hudson River. She loved it. Her dad ran a small beach with camps and a boating operation, a welcomed respite for the businessmen who worked in Albany. These men and their families would go up to their camps at Devoe's Beach ("Pop's" to me) in the summer, their wives and kids lazing the warm slanted days of summer swimming and card playing and exploring the surrounding woods and inlets with the kids of the other camping families. The days passed easily, until dinner, when the dads returned from work and the families gathered and caught up on family matters and the happenings of the day on the River. My mom and her dad would tend to these families and their rowboat rentals, replete with fishing rods and reels and bait.

My mom always spoke lovingly and wistfully of her young girl's days on the River. I always knew she wished she could step right back to her girlhood days on the Hudson instead of sitting in the cramped kitchen in our house in town. The house she grew up in stood on a hill above the River, up a hill so high they never had to worry about flooding, even in the rainiest years. It was a simple house, nothing fancy, and they didn't even have a bathroom. Her baths and the washing of her hair were done in the river, with a bar of soap and a little nighttime cloak or the early morning haze for a bit of privacy. Her memories of river–bathing and tending and swimming swirled around the sunny, breezy days of enjoyable work, companionship, and relaxation. Her girlhood stories were of endless summer and sent a pang to my heart.

My mother swam the River, and I mean she swam *across* the River. Her strength and agility to do such a feat put me in a rare awe. My mother, MY mother, swam across the River; surely not the English Channel, but still, how many girls could say their mother swam *across* the River, not merely in it? I could hardly imagine that my mother had been so young and strong and carefree, let alone *determined* to do such a thing. This story felt like legend, for I could hardly believe that my chubby mother, with her housecoats, dishpan hands, and expansive stomach, could have ever done such an amazing thing! I envisioned trying to swim the River myself, of getting out into the very deep channel and being confronted with one of the "suckers," as we kids called them, the huge barges that sucked the water up off the beach for yards as they chugged by. Everyone left the water when the suckers came; they were that powerful. I did think one day of trying to swim across the River, with someone in a rowboat in case I got a cramp or got too tired, but that was just an *idea*, not something I really intended on doing.

But my mother's legendary swims were held with pride and awe in my heart, especially since I rarely saw her swim when I was a girl. On those rare occasions she did, she would dip her fingers into the water and bless herself. Then, she would walk out into the water and glide in, hitting her strokes evenly and with a precision I never saw in the other bathers. Her swim would be brief, though, and I wondered why she left the water so soon. The swimmer of the River that she once was, the one I wanted to see in real life, I never did see in action.

As my mother aged, and her family home was left to others and then bought by strangers, it still was with longing that she spoke of the Hudson. My mom is now in a nursing home, eighty years old and crippled. When she first was placed there, "rehabilitation" after her hip replacement, we knew it was a permanent placement. My heart is less heavy, though, as in those early nursing home days. I took her out for rides from time to time. I bought coffees, hers black, which we drank, quietly, as we watched the movement of the River from a gazebo overlooking it in my hometown of Schuylerville.

"I have always loved 'My River,'" she said. "Those days were so good." And my heart still pangs. Now, her health deteriorating and her ability to move so limited, I cannot take her out to "Her River" anymore. As she slips further and further into dementia and inertia, I do imagine this legend will find her, at the moment of the ending of her life, once more on the shores of the Hudson. Then, with a quick blessing and graceful glide into the water, she will be carried along its currents of memory, youthful joy, and immortality.

Not Henry Hudson

Sonia T. Lynch

When I sailed into the mighty Hudson River, on August 15, 1961, I felt some of the emotions that Henry Hudson must have encountered on that fateful morning in 1609: wonder, excitement, fear, what am I getting into? And hope.

Hope that this would be a beginning – not an ending; hope that it would be a strong building block between the past and the future; hope that it would be a step upwards on the ladder of life, not down; hope (and fear) whether the natives would prove welcoming and friendly.

Life on the Hudson had changed a little in those three hundred and fifty years. Then the buildings were small and temporary, the inhabitants largely seasonal. There were no travelogues or maps then, no government agencies to decree who could or couldn't set foot on their shores. For me there were visas, passports, luggage regulations, currency and health laws and customs officials to obey. What a difference three hundred years makes.

Then there was no Statue of Liberty. Poor Henry. He didn't have the thrill of his first sight of her, standing there with her flame held high, welcoming the new-comer and proclaiming liberty to the world. There were no skyscrapers, no concrete canyons, no electricity or telephones if he got lost. Even how to calculate longitude when out of sight of land was not known when he arrived.

But the river was here. That immense, enormous width of water, with its tidal flow, changing every six hours; its shores covered with trees, the precipitous rocks rising sheer out of the water, haven't changed. They are just as impressive three hundred years later for a scared newcomer as they would have been for him. His ship was large for its time. Mine also. But he was exploring. He didn't expect to stay. Conversely, I came like a snail, with my house on my back, my green card in my pocket, and unformulated dreams to carry me through those early years. The traditional wide-eyed optimist!

Now, almost fifty years later, I am still looking forward. Grateful for the intervening years of life – filled with happiness and tears, hard work and love, children, family and friends.

I went back and saw the Statue some years ago, on my fortieth anniversary. It was an emotional experience on a beautiful, sunny August day. Three weeks later was 9/11, made all the more emphatic by my recent visit there. But my Statue is still standing at the entrance to Henry's harbor, proudly holding her flame aloft for freedom.

Thank you, Henry, for putting our river on the map. And thank you to those individuals who, in the three hundred and fifty years since he arrived, made it possible for me to come to these shores. And thank you to those who have made me welcome ever since.

Author Biographies

Barbara Adams is the author of two books of poetry and a book of literary criticism on Laura Riding. Her short stories, essays and poems have been published widely in literary and professional magazines. She has also written a play on Sylvia Plath, produced by Mohonk Mountain Stage Company, and reads her work frequently in the Hudson Valley and in New York City. Her poem, "Henry Jones, from Wales," won the 2007 Robert Frost Foundation Award. She was born in Manhattan, lived in New Paltz, and has lived in Newburgh for over 40 years. She considers the Hudson River the most beautiful of all rivers. She retired as Professor of English at Pace University in 2000.

Kevin Larkin Angioli is a poet, musician, and educator who has lived in the Hudson Valley most of his life, delighting in its awesome beauty, spiritual sustenance, and cultural vitality. He has performed his poetry throughout the valley. He is lucky enough to live at the foot of the Shawangunk Mountains.

Laurence Carr writes fiction, poetry and for the theatre. He is the editor of *Riverine: An Anthology of Hudson Valley Writers*, and *The Wytheport Tales*, a volume of micro-fiction, both published by Codhill Press. His writings and plays have been widely published and produced throughout the country and in Europe.

Lucia Cherciu's poetry has appeared in *Riverine: An Anthology of Hudson Valley Writers*, *ESL Magazine,* and in the following Romanian magazines: *Oglinda Literară, Pro Saeculum, Salonul Literar,* and *Astra.* Her book of poetry in Romanian titled "Lepădarea de Limbă" ("The Abandonment of Language") is forthcoming from Editura Vinea. She lives in Poughkeepsie, NY.

Paul Clemente was born and raised on the banks of the Hudson River. He is young enough to have missed Woodstock and old enough to remember the mothballed WW II fleet in Haverstraw Bay. He is a scientist with the NYSDEC. He lives in Esopus with his wife and two sons.

James Finn Cotter is a professor of English at Mount Saint Mary College, Newburgh NY. He is the author of *Inscape: The Christology and Poetry of Gerard Manley Hopkins* and of articles on Dante, Chaucer, Sidney, Hopkins and Salinger. He has translated *The Divine Comedy* published by SUNY Stony Brook. He is president of the International Hopkins Association. His poetry has been published in *America, The Commonweal, The Hudson Review, The Nation, The New York Times, Sparrow, Spirit, Thought,* and other periodicals. He is also the author of *Beginnings: the first Twenty-Five Years of Mount Saint Mary College.*

Joann K. Deiudicibus has always had rivers, first, the Delaware and now, the Wallkill. A writing instructor and Staff Assistant for the Composition Program at SUNY New Paltz, where she received her BA (2000), and MA (2003) in English, Joann has read her poetry to, near, and around the Hudson River since 1995. She has been published in *The North Street Journal, Orange Review, Literary Passions, Fortunate Fall, Chronogram,* and *The Shawangunk Review,* and her poetry was selected for The Woodstock Poetry Festival in 2003.

Lynne Digby has always been involved in the creative arts. She has visual art in the McGraw-Hill collection, and her paintings were used for the first three years on the set of HBO's, "Sex & the City," starring Sarah Jessica Parker. As a co-founder of the Warwick Valley Writers Group, she writes fiction, usually short stories steeped in dark humor. She also has a fantasy novel to her credit that tells how a little cat, through unconditional love saves the planet of Tarrascon. Her book of self-illustrated poetry, *May I Share With You* is now in its third printing.

Thomas Doran is from New Paltz.

Odessa Elliott is the author of *That Much Good Be Done*, a history of a church located in Harriman State Park in Rockland County. She retired as a program associate of the Trinity (Wall St.) Grants Program in New York City.

Allen C. Fischer, former director of marketing for a nationwide corporation, brings to poetry a background in business. A resident of Saugerties, NY, his poems have appeared in *Atlanta Review, Indiana Review, The Laurel Review, Poetry, Prairie Schooner, and Rattle*.

Joe Fischer, j1house@yahoo.com is a singer/songwriter residing in Brooklyn, after over a decade living and performing in Seattle, WA. His music career started in New Paltz, while attending SUNY, as a founding member of the art/rock band CATHOUSE. Besides songs, he is currently writing poems, lyrics and short, comical, semi-autobiographical essays.

Penny A. Freel is a lecturer at SUNY New Paltz. She was born and raised in Poughkeepsie, NY.

Barbara Freer is a freelance writer who lives in Binnewater, NY.

Jonathan M. Freiman was born and raised in New York City. In his youth he spent his summers in and around Columbia County, NY acquiring a fondness for rural settings as a great sanctuary from the urban landscape. He currently resides in South Jersey and frequents his old summer retreat.

Nancy O. Graham's fiction has appeared in *Prima Materia, Café Irreal,* and *Pindeldyboz*, and her poems in *Aught, Chronogram, BlazeVOX*, and *Eratio*. Her chapbook, *somniloquies*, is available from Pudding House. Her blog, *oswegatchie*, is named for the river upstate where her grandmother grew up. She lives in Kingston, NY.

Jim Handlin jhandlin@woodstockdayschool.org . I'm a well published poet – Virginia Quarterly, Poetry, Prairie Schooner, Patterson Literary Review, Lips, etc. I have a poem in marble in Penn Station in Manhattan as part of the new NJ transit terminal along with William Carlos Williams, Walt Whitman, Amiri Baraka, and eight other poets. I have been headmaster of Woodstock Day School for the past two years where I teach poetry to the senior class. I live in Woodstock.

Werner Henst: Born in Germany, I have lived in the US since 1953. I retired from IBM in 1987 and am co-founder and administrator of OUR MONTESSORI SCHOOL in Yorktown. My writing has appeared in *Snowy Egret, Smithsonian, Prima Materia, Riverine* and elsewhere. I live with my wife, Betty, in Somers.

Andrew C. Higgins lives in Kingston, New York and teaches American literature at SUNY New Paltz. His poetry has appeared several journals, including *The New York Quarterly*, *The Paterson Literary Review*, *The Shawangunk Review*, and *Chronogram*. higginsa@newpaltz.edu

Ken Holland has had prose and poetry published in numerous literary journals and have received several awards and grants for my writing, including a Pushcart nomination. I have work forthcoming in *Southwest Review* and *Texas Review*. I work in Manhattan for a publishing company.

Colin Jones is a writer and former student at SUNY New Paltz.

Mike Jurkovic, from Wallkill, co-directs Calling All Poets & hosts the semi-annual Hudson Valley Poets Fest. Published in over seventy literary magazines and three national anthologies, including *Riverine* (Codhill Press, 2007). CD reviews appear in *Elmore Magazine & Folk & Acoustic Music Exchange*. He loves Emily most of all.

Bobbi Katz: Growing up in Newburgh during radio days, I fell in love with words and rhythm. Thanks to Fats Waller, I've made a living as a writer! Harcourt, Harper Collins, Penguin Putnam, among others, publish collections of my poetry for young people. Other credits include a biography, articles, and professional books.

Christine Boyka Kluge is the author of *Stirring the Mirror* and *Teaching Bones to Fly,* both from Bitter Oleander Press. Her chapbook, *Domestic Weather*, won the 2003 Uccelli Press Chapbook Contest. Also a visual artist, she lives in North Salem, New York.

Madeline Mazzetti Labriola: I have lived in the Hudson
Valley for 65 years. I worked in Highland Schools for 25 years
as a teacher and assistant principal. I have 5 children and 10
grandchildren. I currently work at the United Nations as the NGO
head delegate for Pax Christi International, the international
Catholic peace movement.

Nancy Lautenbach is an arts administrator and artist. Her practice
includes work in a variety of media including: pen and ink,
sculpture, ceramics, installation, photography, and bookmaking
with current work focusing on her passion for the environment and
the feminine connection of woman to nature.

Donald Lev lives in High Falls, NY where he edits and publishes
Home Planet News, the arts tabloid he and his late wife, Enid
Dame, founded in 1979. His poetry has been widely published in
periodicals and anthologies and fourteen collections of his poetry
have been published since 1968.

Michael Lutomski has lived in New Paltz for the past five years,
but the Hudson Valley all his twenty seven. He received his BA
from SUNY New Paltz, minoring in creative writing and majoring
in English. He is currently in the Master's program at SUNY
New Paltz, again majoring in English, and teaching Freshman
Composition through the Teaching Assistant program. His work
has been published in the "Literary Gazette" of the *River Reporter*
and the *Shawangunk Review*.

Sonia Lynch was born outside London. The family moved to the
countryside when she was five. She worked in London before
coming to America where she met her husband. After daughters
were born, a divorce, an Economics degree from SUNY Purchase
and a lifetime in Accounting, she now enjoys writing.

Judy Mage: I grew up in the Bronx, and graduated from Antioch
College. In 1966 I was elected president of the union I'd helped
organize in the NYC Welfare Department. In 1970, I moved to
Ulster County, where my son was born. I was a Social Worker for
Ulster BOCES and live in New Paltz.

Mary Armao McCarthy is past president of the Hudson Valley Writers Guild. Her essays and poetry have appeared in anthologies, periodicals, online magazines, and public radio. Recent books include *Aunties: 35 Writers Celebrate Their Other Mothers* and *Voices of Breast Cancer.* She has worked in education, government, and pubic policy.

Betsy McCully's most recent book is *City at the Water's Edge: A Natural History of New York* (Rivergate, 2007), based on fifteen years of research and nature exploration in her adopted city, where she has lived now for 25 years. She is an Associate Professor of English at Kingsborough Community College.

Meg McKay is a student at Marist College.

Claudia McQuistion: In May 2007, I graduated from Clark University in Massachusetts. I am from Hastings-on-Hudson, but have been living in Seattle for a little over a year. My poetry has appeared in *Fifth Wednesday Journal.*

Patricia Martin: A native of CT, Patricia Martin moved to the Hudson Valley two decades ago after falling in love with it. She is a published author, poet, performer, and freelance copywriter who now lives in West Saugerties.

Marion Menna: I am a retired Long Island special ed teacher, now living in Glenmont, New York. I am a volunteer naturalist at Five Rivers Nature Center and AIHA. I have had poems published in *Walt Whitman Birthplace, Avocet, and Stone Canoe II.* My first chapbook will be forthcoming in June, 2009.

Robert Milby, of Florida, NY has been reading his work in the Hudson Valley, NYC, Long Island, NJ, PA, and New England since March, 1995. Published in: *Home Planet News, Riverine (anthology) Hunger Magazine, Chronogram, Hudson Valley Literary Magazine, Will Work For Peace(anthology), Soul Fountain, Asbestos*, OTHER: the Albany Poets Magazine, *Metroland, Core Pieces, many more both in print and online. His*

first book of poetry is Ophelia's Offspring (Foothills Publishing, Kanona, NY 2007) His spoken word CD is Revenant Echo (Sonotrope Recordings, High Falls, NY 2004) He is a listed poet with Poets & Writers, Inc. of NYC. Robert writes for *The Delaware and Hudson Canvas*, in Bloomingburgh, NY, and hosts 6 Hudson Valley poetry readings.
www.robertmilby.com

Pam Mitchell is a psychiatric nurse now living on the Deschutes River in Bend, OR after many years in Saratoga Springs, NY. Her love of rivers runs deep, having spent many hours in her Hornbeck boat traveling and listening to the wisdom of the waters. Recently some water broke, and she helped deliver her first granddaughter.

Jack Murphy: I came to New Paltz in 1967 to attend college and received a Bachelor of Fine Arts degree in Photography. My photographs have been exhibited and published. I am the Web Coordinator for Ulster County Community College. I build and play cigar box guitars and other hand made stringed instruments.

Janet Neipris has had plays produced at major theatres in the U.S. and internationally. Her award winning play, *A Small Delegation*, was named one of the best plays of the year by *The Philadelphia Enquirer,* (Annenberg Center production), one of the best plays by women (Studio Theatre, D.C. production), and was produced in the U.S. and Beijing. Chair of the Graduate Playwriting and Screenwriting Dept., Dramatic Writing, NYU's Tisch School of the Arts, she has educated some of the country's leading playwrights. Her book, *To Be A Playwright,* was published in 2005 by Routledge. She has been a member of the Dramatists Guild Council, Tony Committee, Writer's Guild of America, East, and PEN.

Hideichi Oshiro is a resident of the city of Newburgh. At 98 years of age, he continues to write Haiku and draw every day. In the over 60 years of his collected works, one can witness the vast reaches of this writer, philosopher and artist's mind.

Thomas Perkins was born in Brooklyn, New York in 1969. It was, however, the New Jersey suburb where he was raised that inspired him to join the Peace Corps in search of some…flavor. After four years of increasing fluency in Thailand, he fell in love and started the family with whom he has been globe trotting ever since. As the Perkins family plans to move to their new home on Cantine's Island in Saugerties, Thomas hopes for something his poetry has been sadly lacking: a community with which to share it and by which it may grow. http://wisage7.blogspot.com/.

Jo Pitkin received an M.F.A. from the University of Iowa. Her poems were published in *The Measure* (Finishing Line Press) and *Ironwood, Quarterly West, Nimrod, Vanguard Voices of the Hudson Valley – Poetry 2007, Riverine, Stone Canoe*, and others. She lives in Cold Spring in a former schoolhouse built in 1830.

Marilyn Reynolds recently published in the *Riverine* anthology. I continue to live parallel lives in writing and the visual arts. I have received many grants, and opportunities, including a residency at the MacDowell Colony in New Hampshire. I am, as well, Director of Arts in Education at the Caramoor Center for Music and the Arts.

Abigail Robin is a teacher and writer residing in Kingston, NY. Her memoir, *L'Chaim*, has recently been published. She teaches at SUNY New Paltz.

Anthony Robinson, Professor (emeritus) of English at SUNY New Paltz and author of five novels, grew up in Woodstock, NY. Except for a three-year tour in the U.S. Navy during Korea, he has lived his entire life in the Hudson valley; now, with his wife Tania, on Huguenot Street in New Paltz.

Annajon Russ is the pen name of Anne Richey of Hurley, NY. Her poems have appeared in national and regional journals. Lately, she has been channeling the Chinese poet Li Po (701-762 CE). "On Overlook Mountain with the Rock Reader" was written after a hike with Robert Titus, a Catskills geologist.

Judith Saunders teaches at Marist College. Her poems have been published in *Chronogram, Oxalis, The Hudson Valley Review, Poet Magazine* and *Thelma*, among others.

William Seaton is a poet, translator, and scholar who lives in Goshen, New York. His most recent publications are *Spoor of Desire: Selected Poems* and *Tourist Snapshots*. Seaton has produced the Poetry on the Loose Reading/Performance series in the Hudson Valley since 1993.

Jan Zlotnik Schmidt is a SUNY Distinguished Teaching Professor in the Department of English at SUNY New Paltz. Her poetry has been published in *Kansas Quarterly, Cream City Review, Syracuse Scholar, Alaska Quarterly Review, Home Planet News*, and *Phoebe*. She has published two volumes of poetry: *We Speak in Tongues* and *She had this memory* (Edwin Mellen Press, 1991) and two collections of autobiographical essays: *Women/Writing/Teaching* (SUNY Press 1998) and *Wise Women: Reflections of Teachers in Midlife*, co-authored with Dr. Phyllis Freeman (Routledge 2000).

Rhonda Shary has lived and worked in the lower Hudson River Valley since 1998. Prior to that, she lived and worked in New York City, where her daughter was born in a room at St. Vincent's Hospital overlooking the Hudson River; and in Columbus, Ohio, near the Ohio and Olentangy Rivers. She currently teaches at SUNY New Paltz.

Donna Sherman: I've worked as a psychotherapist and health educator for over 25 years and have been writing poetry, verse and short essays for about as many years. After 20 years of living in Princeton, NJ, my family and I have relocated to New Paltz where we spend a good deal of time hiking and exploring the banks of the Hudson. Since this past spring I have had the pleasure of working as an occasional environmental educator with Clearwater. In short, I love the river: its history, its stunning beauty and its ever-changing textures.

James Sherwood resides in New Paltz, a TA/Graduate student (May 2009) in the English department at SUNY New Paltz, as well as a member of the Poetry Board. Originally from Long Island, now a happy transplant to the Hudson Valley, intending to stay and grow in that rich soil.

Linda J. Still was raised in Schuylerville, a mill town on the Hudson in Saratoga County. There, in the Adirondacks' foothills, the River is not as expansive as here in the Hudson Valley, where she's lived for 25 years. But its power and majesty and calling are no less apparent.

Joanne Rose Trapanese: I've loved the Hudson Valley for many years. I grew up in Yonkers, not far from the Hudson River, and I've lived in Columbia County for the past 24 years. The beauty of this valley never ceases to amaze and delight me.

Maureen Waters: I've enjoyed living in the Hudson Valley for over 30 years; certainly the experience has influenced my writing as well as my perspective on life. I've published three books--the last a prize-wining memoir, Crossing Highbridge, as well as poetry, essays, reviews. Most of my professional life was spent at Queens College, CUNY, teaching Irish Studies.

Robert H. Waugh: I have lived in the New Paltz area for over forty years, having taught in the English Department at SUNY New Paltz since 1968. Since last year I now live in Port Ewen, looking down on the Rondout. After publishing many essays and poems over the years in various scholarly journals and small magazines, I recently finished a book on H. P. Lovecraft called *The Monster in the Mirror* and a chapbook called *Shorewards, Tidewards*.

Ethel Wesdorp is a quilter, dancer and writer living in Saugerties, NY.

Chelsea Whitaker is a Hudson Valley student writer. She plans on becoming a novelist in the future and would like to attend college in Massachusetts. She will be traveling through Europe in the summer of 2010 to broaden her experiences with different cultures and prepare for a career in writing.

Tyler Wilhelm, author of *Alive*: a collection of poetry available from Liberty Artists publications (libertyartists.com)

A. J. Williams-Myers is Professor of African and African American History in the Black Studies Department at SUNY-New Paltz. He holds the doctorate from UCLA, and his archival and field work were done in England, Portugal, Italy, and Zambia, Central Africa with the support of a Ford Foundation Fellowship. Among his publications is his professor-student project, In Their Own Words Voices From the Middle Passage (Africa World Press, Inc.:Trenton, N.J., 2009).

Amelia B. Winkler's articles and essays have appeared in *Jewish Week,* the Westchester section of *The New York Times, North County News* and *Women's News;* her poems have appeared in *Jewish Currents, Red Owl, The Westchester Review* and other small presses. She has a BA in French Literature from Barnard College.

Howard Winn: I am a faculty member at SUNY Dutchess where I have taught fiction and poetry writing. I have a graduate degree from the Stanford University Writing Program where I studied with Yvor Winters and Wallace Stegner. My writing has appeared in numerous publications.

Caroline Wolfe is the creative voice of writer, Marcia Roth Tucci, a composition instructor and advisor at SUNY New Paltz. The author lives in Washingtonville, NY, next to wetlands that feed Moodna Creek and the Hudson River estuary. Caroline Wolfe's essays are published quarterly at www.moondance.org an on-line literary journal.

Bob Wright, who currently resides in Athens, New York, is one of the founders of the Woodstock Poetry Society and for six years served as its coordinator. He has been published in such diverse periodicals as Oxalis, Yankee, the Christian Science Monitor, Freefall Magazine, Heliotrope, and the North Dakota Quarterly and is the curator for the Hudson Valley Poetry Calendar www.poetz. com/hudson